MINDFULNESS WORKBOOK FOR BEGINNERS

MINDFULNESS WORKBOOK
for Beginners

Exercises and Meditations to Relieve
Stress, Find Joy, and Cultivate Gratitude

Peter J. Economou, PhD, ABPP

**ROCKRIDGE
PRESS**

Interior and Cover Designer: Julie Schrader
Art Producer: Sue Bischofberger
Editors: Samantha Barbaro and Crystal Nero
Production Editor: Rachel Taenzler
Illustration © mr_owlman/shutterstock.com, p. 8; Fotini Tikkou, pp. 23, 36, and 105; Amanda Leon, pp. 37 and 57; PaintDoor/shutterstock.com, p. 77; Emila/shutterstock.com, p. 104; all other illustrations used under license from iStock.com
Author photo courtesy of Leigh Castelli Photography

ISBN: Print 978-1-64876-612-1 | eBook 978-1-64876-401-1
R0

A message from Dr. Pete:

To all those who are suffering: May we find peace.

CONTENTS

INTRODUCTION AND HOW TO USE THIS BOOK

Beginning a mindfulness practice is a lot like learning how to ride a bike. No one is born knowing how to ride a bike; instead, we start with training wheels, we fall a few times, and after much practice and concentration, we are eventually able to ride freely. We may feel excitement, nervousness, fear, or other emotions as we try, fail, and learn. Though mindfulness doesn't involve any helmets or scraped knees, beginning a mindfulness practice *will* involve excitement, nervousness, and a lot of concentration. As you learn, you will experience some metaphorical falls. And, just like with that bike so many years ago, it's critical that you get back on and keep riding.

This book is for beginners and for those with curiosity about mindfulness, a practice that teaches us how to manage all kinds of emotions and monitor our reactions to a variety of situations. These situations could include dealing with a difficult boss or family member, coping with the loss of a loved one, living through a global crisis, or stubbing your toe. The benefits of mindfulness are immense, and the practice creates curiosity and acceptance along the spectrum of life's challenges, no matter how big or small.

In Part 1, we will start by delving into what mindfulness actually is and exploring its basic principles. We'll also learn specific uses of mindfulness in managing emotions like anxiety and anger. In Part 2, we will dive deeper into the core and higher-level benefits of the practice of mindfulness, such as gratitude, joy, peace, and kindness. Each chapter will include exercises and opportunities to practice mindfulness. Take your time and be patient with those practices. Some of the exercises will be completed on the page, while others will ask you to go out into nature, move your body, or engage in quiet, internal practices. To develop a steady and manageable mindfulness practice, you might consider creating a schedule guiding when and how you will read this book (e.g., reading one chapter per week and completing two exercises per day is a good pace). I recommend that you complete each section in order.

I began my own journey of mindful living in college, where I competed as an elite swimmer at the highest levels. I then continued my journey in graduate school, perhaps out of survival and necessity. Today, I am a licensed psychologist, professor, and dharma holder. I have formalized my mindfulness practice through years of meditation and studying within the Zen Buddhist traditions. My formal training is in counseling psychology, and I began studying Zen Buddhism in the White Plum lineage under Robert Kennedy Roshi as we shifted into the 21st century. Even now, decades into my mindfulness journey, I find that there are still new things to learn.

The most critical part of this practice is noticing where we are, committing to getting to where we want to be, and practicing the behaviors we need in order to get there. No one is born knowing how to walk; we must first crawl, stand, and stumble. We will also fall often. The key is that we get back up. Now, let's get ready to crawl.

The real meditation is how we live our lives from moment to moment.

—Jon Kabat-Zinn, 2014

PART 1

GETTING STARTED

A life lived mindfully is spent learning to observe and participate in the journey. We learn to view pain and suffering as bystanders, like fans at our favorite team's stadium. Part 1 will begin by broadly defining the practice of mindfulness and where it comes from. Then, we will look at specific issues, like depression, anxiety, and trauma, and how the practice of mindfulness can change those experiences. The practice of mindfulness is a lifelong process—a marathon, not a sprint—and opening this book is the first step.

Chapter 1

WELCOME TO MINDFULNESS

Mindfulness is a practice as well as a lifestyle. When mindfulness is integrated into your routine as deeply as brushing your teeth, you can live with more calm. People who practice mindfulness tend to let go of issues and worry less. That is because mindfulness places the emphasis on living for today, in this present moment. As mindfulness writer and teacher Jon Kabat-Zinn said, mindfulness means you focus on what is happening now, practice nonjudgment, and do whatever you are doing with intention and purpose.

This definition will make more sense as we move through this chapter, which looks at the components and history of mindfulness. Consider this explanation your first mindfulness practice in this workbook: accept that everything you read might not make total sense in *this* exact moment, but read on anyway.

WHAT IS MINDFULNESS?

Jon Kabat-Zinn defined mindfulness as the state of performing an action on purpose, in the present moment and without judgment. Rooted in Buddhist thought, mindfulness is thinking before speaking, acting with awareness, creating inner peace and calm, and changing our brain structures to manage life more effectively, per an article in *Neuroscience*. The practice of mindfulness is not religious or spiritual (unless you want it to be); rather, it works to generate a connection to the life you are living. This means that mindfulness practitioners experience emotions—good, bad, and indifferent—in a more meaningful way and foster deeper relationships. A bonus of practicing mindfulness is that it also enhances relationships and creates a loving relationship with the self. We acknowledge that we all have strengths and weaknesses and we all have experienced pain.

We will develop these concepts in later chapters, but let's first break down the definition of mindfulness.

Purpose

When you think about what it means to do something on purpose, consider the intentions you have as you complete an action. Have you ever *just* peeled a potato? The answer is likely no; when we cook, we are often thinking of many other things. When you peel a potato, you might be thinking about what temperature you need to preheat the oven to in order to cook the rest of your meal, or the person you are cooking for. You could be rehashing an argument you had with a coworker earlier in the day or experiencing some anticipatory anxiety about a flight you're taking tomorrow. Mindfulness is the opposite of this. Within the practice of mindfulness, the goal is to openly commit to our action for the sake of that action—to just peel the potato.

Anything can be mindful if you do it with purpose, even running errands. Say you're driving to the bank. You pull into the parking lot and notice one spot that is close to the ATM and several others that are much farther away. You are trying to be more active for your health, but taking the closer spot would be easier. Taking the close spot would not be doing something with purpose; it would simply be taking the easier option, one that does not have anything to do with your intention. However, acknowledging the close spot, parking farther away, and walking is a decision made with intention.

Doing things with purpose requires that you reflect on your motivation to complete the task. You listen to the thoughts that are driving you there, you are able to describe your emotions during that experience, and there is no deception. The truth is that we cannot deceive ourselves. When I park close to the ATM because I am being lazy, I cannot hide from that. We know what we are doing, when we are doing it, and why it is important. The practice of mindfulness raises our awareness to the senses during our experiences.

Present Moment

One of the fundamental teachings of Buddhism is there is no period of time other than *this* moment. Pain is often caused by a memory from the past or a worry related to the future. The practice of mindfulness encourages us to find existence in this present moment. Say you are waiting in line to check out at the grocery store and you are late to meet a friend. As you get emotionally activated (i.e., feel anxiety about your friend's reaction, frustration about the line, and maybe even anger at the cashier for taking so long), you are likely responding to shame about how this friend has told you that you are "always late" (past) or worries about traffic and other issues that could make you even later (future). Present moment living would just have you focus on the inhale and the exhale and on your feet on the ground, in that line with your items. *Whenever you get to meet your friend is when you will get there.* Getting all worked up in this moment does not change the fact that you may be late *again*.

Think about cooking a meal of salmon, mashed potatoes, and asparagus. (Notice if you salivated at all while reading that menu; that is the power of the mind and body.) To prepare the meal, you have to preheat the oven, clean the salmon, prep the skillet for the asparagus, and peel the potatoes. Often, as we cook, we worry about whether people will like the food, fear that we will overcook the salmon, or hold on to a feeling or interaction from earlier in the day. But present moment living is *just* peeling the potatoes. When you turn the oven on, do so in that moment. Then, when you're by the sink with the salmon, just be there. Develop a plan. Then, as you take each action needed to execute that plan, just do that action. We will learn more about this in chapter 3.

Nonjudgment

Try walking into a store, having a conversation with a relative, or playing a pick-up basketball game *without* judging the store, the relative, or the opponents. It is impossible. Neuroscientist and philosopher Joshua Greene said that judgment is one of the key characteristics of the human experience. When you walk into the store, you notice the employees, the smells and sounds, the color and aesthetics of the decor, and the sound of the music they're playing. All of your senses are involved. How can you do that without judgment? It is basically impossible; humans are hardwired to judge experiences. This is what has kept us safe and alive since the dawn of human existence. What if there were a saber-toothed tiger outside on the front lawn? As cute as it might be, I would need to judge it and the situation before becoming the tiger's lunch.

Nonjudgment doesn't mean that you must stop judging people, things, or experiences. Rather, the *nonjudgment* part of mindfulness challenges you to notice judgments, in an effort to work toward neutral judgment of experiences. In the case of the saber-toothed tiger; neutral judgment states, "There is a saber-toothed tiger on my lawn." This neutral judgment describes what is, rather than using other adjectives like "cute," "strong," "weak," "dangerous," or "hungry."

Neutral judgment does not mean that we interact with the tiger. We simply describe our experiences. Here is another example: you could judge this as the best workbook ever or the worst workbook ever. However, the neutral judgment would be, simply, that this is a mindfulness workbook for beginners. In the practice of mindfulness, our goal is to notice the judgments that are natural to the human experience, observe them, and commit to neutral judgment of our experiences. We will also learn more about this in chapter 3.

In summary, mindfulness is a way of living life fully. I find that people become overwhelmed initially with these practices, which makes sense; the mind and our emotions are loud. That's why the famous Buddhist writer and psychologist Eckhart Tolle titled one of his books *Stillness Speaks*. It is true that when you slow down and listen to your mind and heart, the volume of your experiences gets turned up. I encourage people to consider mindfulness in the same way you would consider whether you are tall or short or a righty, a lefty, or ambidextrous; the practice of mindfulness becomes a part of you. Do not impose it on others, and for those who do not understand mindful living, practice acceptance and compassion. (You will learn more about this in later chapters.) It's also important to recognize that there are times when you will slip up. Like any relationship in life, there are ups and downs. With a mindful approach, the ups and downs are smoothed out and our experiences are more enjoyable.

What Mindfulness Is Not

Mindfulness is whatever you want it to be. It could be walking your dog in the morning, a formal meditation practice, emotional vulnerability with a supervisor or family member, gardening, a yoga practice, or countless other expressions.

Anyone in any situation can become mindful without changing their religious affiliation or other beliefs. You do not need to take any vows or go through a bonding ceremony. You simply have to be curious, willing to ride the waves, practice patience, and notice opportunities for courage. I consider this an evolution in your life at this place and time.

Mindfulness is not quick; rather, it is like building a muscle. If you want to build up your biceps, you would not expect to work out once and be done with it. Instead, you would have to increase weight, increase reps over time, and practice with a committed schedule. That is mindfulness. Opening this book is starting with the desire to build muscle; throughout the chapters, you will be increasing the reps and the weight. By the end of the book, you will be stronger. But I cannot promise your biceps will be as big as you want them to be.

The practice of mindfulness doesn't change who you are. I had a client once ask me, "Dr. Pete, do you expect I will be wearing sandals and lighting incense after working with you?" She liked expensive things and was always dressed very nicely. I responded that she could be whoever she wanted to be—that is the beauty of mindfulness. As you progress with the practice of mindfulness, you will maintain your personality and the characteristics of who you are. There may be times when you might enhance qualities that you love about yourself and consider changing those things that you do not love as much. But your outer self does not have to change. Instead, you will build a stronger relationship with the inner self and be less affected by situations that typically negatively impact you.

Mindful Origins

To truly understand the practice of mindfulness, we must look at its Buddhist origin. Thousands of years ago, Buddhist scholars acknowledged that everyone suffered, and they found that much of the suffering was created by ignorance and greed. Ignorance in this case meant ignoring one's emotions and the needs of one's community; greed related to the attachment to material things. These teachings produced the Four Noble Truths, which are defined in Heinrich Dumoulin's *Zen Buddhism*. The First Noble Truth claims that suffering is universal. The goal is to relieve that suffering through non-attachment (Second Noble Truth). We then acknowledge that there is a way to release suffering: by living fully and by not desiring (Third Noble Truth). Finally, the Eightfold Path teaches us how to live (Fourth Noble Truth). It is important to have a cursory understanding of these eight actions, but note that this is a condensed and brief description.

The Eightfold Path involves developing the right view, resolve, speech, conduct, livelihood, effort, mindfulness, and meditation (or *samadhi*). Put simply, it is thinking before speaking, taking action with a moral compass that considers the consequences, and committing to curiosity in this life.

Always a Beginner

In mindfulness, we all have a *beginner's mind*: we see things as they are for the first time each time we see them. It's like walking around your hometown with a tourist and seeing things as if you had never seen them before. We do not have to be experts in anything. We are just open to this experience in this moment. You do not need to answer questions related to "why." You have permission to not know.

MINDFULNESS BENEFITS

In my experience, mindfulness can be beneficial for any person, as long as they're ready and willing to practice it. Even if you find that you do not suffer much and are generally content, the practice of mindfulness can enhance your life, helping reduce stress; improve your focus, self-control, and memory; and create greater overall happiness and confidence.

But if you are dealing with a particular mental health issue, such as anxiety or depression, mindfulness offers proven benefits for managing symptoms. In the following sections, I will briefly explain the positive effects of a mindfulness practice for those dealing with anxiety, stress, trauma, and depression. I'll also examine how mindfulness can help you improve your self-esteem and self-confidence, as well as manage anger and other strong emotions.

However, this book is not a substitute for therapy or other mental health support. Rather, it can be used after successfully completing therapy or in conjunction with a trained practitioner. As a psychologist who is board certified in cognitive and behavioral therapy (CBT), a certified mental performance consultant (CMPC), and a student of Zen, many of the clinical interventions I use are evidence-based and stem from mindfulness-based principles. Mindfulness works and it can change lives for the better, but this book is meant to guide; it is not meant to replace professional mental health treatment.

Anxiety and Stress

Everyone feels anxiety—it's one of the six basic emotions, according to Dr. Paul Ekman. However, when experienced in excess, it can be debilitating and have negative effects on life. Stress, another universal experience, can also negatively impact your well-being. People dealing with excessive anxiety and stress may experience issues with sleep, changes in appetite, digestive problems, back pain, headaches, challenges with relationships, and difficulty controlling negative emotions such as irritability. Mindfulness can and does help.

Jon Kabat-Zinn developed a technique called Mindfulness-Based Stress Reduction (MBSR) while working with patients with chronic pain. Today, MBSR is shown to be an effective tool for coping with a variety of issues, including anxiety and stress. In 2013, the first empirical study on the practice found that mindfulness meditation lowered reported anxiety symptoms. Researchers have also found that these mindfulness-based practices enhance brain structures such as the insula cortex and amygdala, which are responsible for emotion regulation and sense of self, and even reduce stress-inducing hormones like adrenocorticotropic hormone. Readers seeking relief in this area will especially benefit from chapter 7.

Trauma

Research published in the *Journal of Traumatic Stress* has found that nearly 10% of the general population in the United States will experience trauma affecting their psychological functioning during their lifetime. I suspect that, based on recent events in the 21st century (including the COVID-19 global pandemic), these numbers are likely higher. Mental health professionals can assess whether these traumatic events cause enough significant changes to one's ability to exist in the world to meet criteria for post-traumatic stress disorder (PTSD).

Mindfulness practices can assist with managing trauma. In 2018, a study found that meditating reduced trauma-related symptoms such as nightmares, hypervigilance, and signs of depression. Another study found MBSR to be an effective treatment regimen for women who experienced trauma related to family violence, childhood physical or sexual abuse, or the sudden loss of a loved one. The MBSR protocol is used throughout this book, as it is a highly studied program that works (see the Resources section, page 161, for more information). Readers seeking relief in this area will especially benefit from chapter 6.

Depression

Depression, just like anxiety, is a common and natural emotion. We all feel sadness from time to time when we lose a loved one or a pet, end a career or friendship, or experience an unexpected setback. But sustained, ongoing depression can drastically lower your quality of life, and many people who experience depression struggle to find a treatment that works. The World Health Organization (WHO) reported that 264 million people globally experience depression and it is the leading cause of disability worldwide.

Mindfulness-based interventions including MBSR, Mindfulness-Based Cognitive Therapy (MBCT), a one-week mindfulness program, and mindfulness meditation have all been shown to help people struggling with depression improve their symptoms. (Each of these techniques is incorporated into this book.) The practice of mindfulness has been shown to be an effective treatment to reduce depressive symptoms for individuals diagnosed with Major Depressive Disorder (MDD). It has also been shown to reduce depression in individuals with Autism Spectrum Disorder. Mindfulness can lead to an overall decrease in symptoms of anxiety and depression for anyone dealing with those issues. Mindfulness-based interventions not only can reduce depression but also can change brain structures such as the precuneus. Within the mindfulness model, it does not necessarily matter where the depression comes from. We do not need to justify the emotion or identify one event that caused it. Readers who wish to address depression would benefit from chapter 9, which focuses on creating joy.

Self-Esteem and Self-Confidence

In today's world, self-esteem and self-confidence levels are low. Social comparison is ubiquitous, especially with the omnipresence of social media, even though most social media posts portray a stylized image rather than a reality. Sociologist Morris Rosenberg determined that several factors contribute to self-esteem, such as genetics, personality styles, overall health, thoughts, social circumstances, how we respond to others, and comparing ourselves to others.

Mindfulness can strengthen all these areas, improving self-esteem in the process. Thompson and Waltz found that practicing mindfulness increased self-acceptance and self-esteem. In another study by Morley and Fulton, researchers found that the integration of mindfulness-based practices made a positive impact on prison inmates' self-esteem and self-compassion. Many of these compassion-based practices focus on gratitude. Readers wishing to increase and focus on self-esteem and self-confidence will benefit from chapter 8, which focuses on practicing gratitude.

Anger and Other Strong Emotions

Anger is another common and basic emotion. It is adaptive to some extent, meaning that it serves a purpose (for example, to prevent someone from manipulating or using you). Our focus within mindfulness practices is to create space for anger.

One common aspect of anger is constant thinking, which in psychology is called *rumination*. One 2020 study found that individuals who practiced mindfulness were able to interrupt the rumination, thus creating space for anger management. Mindfulness is not anger cessation; it is acknowledging that we need to manage the emotion because we will likely never be able to eliminate it.

That is the main focus of mindfulness and these sections related to specific challenges: we aim to modulate, manage, and interact with our challenging emotions. We cannot remove them. Readers who want to deal with strong emotions or emotional volatility will benefit from chapter 10.

THE HOW-TO OF MINDFULNESS

> *To live is to suffer, to survive is to find some meaning in the suffering.* —Gordon Allport, PhD

This quote from Allport is also true in the practice of mindfulness and the Buddhist teachings of suffering. If mindfulness were easy, I believe that more people would be doing it, because it offers so many benefits. But mindfulness is not easy. However, neither are most valuable pursuits.

Common Terms

Anticipatory anxiety: The jittery feelings one might experience leading up to an anxiety-provoking event or interaction.

Cognitive flexibility: Awareness of thought and openness to how others think.

Curiosity and openness: A state of feeling nonjudgmental, flexible, open to creative thinking, and willing to try new things.

Dialectic: Bridging two opposing forces, synthesizing the thesis and the antithesis.

Intention: Acknowledgment of the purpose of an action, thought, or speech.

Mindfulness: The state of performing an action on purpose, in the present moment, and without judgment.

Nonjudgment: Observing and describing experiences, emotions, and interactions from a neutral perspective.

Present moment: Here and now.

Psychological flexibility: Awareness of emotion and openness to others' emotions.

Six basic emotions: Sadness, happiness, fear, anger, surprise, and disgust.

Zen Buddhism: A Japanese sect of Mahayana Buddhism focused on meditation and intuition.

As long as you remain curious, open, and nonjudgmental, you will see benefits (even though we typically do not approach these practices with that end goal in mind, or even the goal of feeling better). Please continue to practice openness to each mindfulness activity, develop your own pace, notice when and where you find yourself frustrated or stuck, and acknowledge that you have made this first step to mindful living by opening this book.

Essential Components

As we consider what it means to be in this present moment, without judgment and with intention, let us first look at some basic yet important components of mindfulness. I have found that the most essential parts of cultivating a mindfulness practice are psychological and cognitive flexibility. Psychological flexibility is awareness of your emotions, and cognitive flexibility is awareness of your thoughts. Awareness of your emotions and thoughts creates the openness needed to begin these mindful practices. This openness and awareness allow us to recognize the positive and negative aspects of this present moment, defuse judgment, and create action in an intentional manner.

Building Your Practice

There really is no right or wrong way to begin the practice of mindfulness. However, I have learned some skills that foster a strong practice with both flexibility and commitment. Much of this practice is similar to other relationships in your life; there are moments when they are super strong and other times when you feel those same relationships are holding on by a thread. Accept that you will have periods in your life when you cannot get enough of these practices and other times when you will be watching the clock.

For starters, commit to a daily practice. This can begin small—even just one or two minutes per day works. You could even plan to practice mindfulness while doing a daily chore, like brushing your teeth. Gradually and slowly add time, with the hope of eventually practicing for 30 minutes per day.

Then, create a space for silent sitting. Silent sitting is when you sit with your knees directly above your opposite ankles (or cross-legged on the floor or a cushion), shoulders above your hips, and the crown of your head to the ceiling. You can close your eyes or you can watch the floor in front of you. Once you are in position, just sit. Some people notice their breath, others pray or repeat a phrase, and some find a space where they can quiet their thoughts. Make sure that your silent sitting space is in an area that is not related to anything else. For example, you do not want to use your desk chair since that is related to work, and you do not want to use your bed because the body sees that as a place for sleep or intimacy.

Finally, raise your awareness of your judgments by writing them down when they happen. This can be while you are practicing and judging me as the author for a "silly exercise" or when you are shopping, interacting with a loved one, or having a difficult conversation with a coworker. Simply write them in your phone or on a piece of paper. Just the act of writing them down raises awareness and attention. Subsequently, we notice them more and then judge less.

Mindful Brushing

As I mentioned earlier, you can practice mindfulness while doing something as simple as brushing your teeth. How? Just brush your teeth. Listen to the water, smell the toothpaste, feel the bristles on your teeth, consider the evolution of your teeth from dirty to clean as you brush, and just brush. Each time your mind wanders and you begin to think about the past day or tomorrow, bring it back to brushing.

How Often and How Much?

Living mindfully is not easy (at least not at first). If you were not raised in a culture with a strong Buddhist heritage, you are probably conditioned to live life with higher intensity. Switching from that to mindfulness may feel strange at first, like trying to write something with your nondominant hand. But just like writing with your other hand, the more you practice, the easier and more comfortable it will get.

What to Expect

One principle of practicing mindfulness-based interventions is that while we want to decrease suffering and angst, the treatment goal is to commit to the practice of mindfulness, develop curiosity, and be patient. Some readers will enjoy the practices immediately and feel connected to them. Others will feel like they could take the practice or leave it. Some will feel frustrated. Please observe where you are; this will help you become unstuck. It will get easier as you progress, and you will begin to see benefits.

When I first started my mindfulness journey, it felt like a chore. I had to remind myself to practice. This isn't uncommon; many clients put reminders in their calendars. Some clients practice daily, some practice weekly, and others practice infrequently. See what works for you, but please commit to the exercises. You know what motivates you, so mindfully use that to stick to these practices. For example, when I first started meditating, I did not like it. It made me anxious. So, I found a community where I could sit with others, which helped to create some accountability. Getting involved in a community, telling loved ones about this commitment to mindful living, or writing sticky note reminders around your home might help you stick with these practices.

There will be times when you feel bored and frustrated and times when you want to rush to the next exercise so that you can get closer to the end. With commitment I believe that you will find some added peace in your life and that you may begin to feel more joy.

Anytime, Anywhere

As you can probably tell, you do not need any kind of expensive membership or fancy equipment to practice mindfulness. You can practice mindfulness anytime, anywhere. If you are having a restless night of sleep, get out of bed, sit on a chair, and take 10 deep belly breaths. When you are riding in a car or train, exercising outside or in the house, in a small meeting at work, or performing your year-end presentation to 350 colleagues, these are all opportunities to practice mindfulness. A colleague of mine has said, "Hope is in the struggle." I remain hopeful that my commitment to teaching the practice of mindfulness will provide others with increased joy and that you have taken that first step to living more deeply.

You have opened this book and read through the first chapter; that is achievement in and of itself. You have likely felt an array of emotions, from optimism to pessimism and from excitement to frustration to hope. Now is the time to consider building this house, one brick at a time.

Chapter 2

STARTING YOUR PRACTICE

What is one of the first things you do when you get home or step into your car? I find that a large percentage of folks put on music or the television. We do things like this because we are distracting from the self and trying to avoid our thoughts and feelings. But the truth is that no matter how loud we turn up the music or the television, we are still there. So, let us build a relationship with ourselves.

THE BUILDING BLOCKS OF MINDFULNESS

In chapter 1, we covered what exactly mindfulness means and explored a few of the basic building blocks of practice. Now, we're going to look a bit more closely at some of the other basic building blocks of mindfulness: attentional breathing, awareness and insight into one's experiences, taking moments to pause and slow down, and connecting with one's values or defining spirituality.

Attentional breathing: I have noticed that when I am in an argument with a loved one, shifting my focus onto my breath can be very helpful. When I do this, I've been able to calmly listen, rather than pouncing and trying to win. Pema Chödrön, a Buddhist monk and author, has written extensively on the power of the breath. In fact, she claims that six breaths can change one's mood and mind-set. Explore this by taking six breaths right now. Push your belly out on the inhale and bring your belly button to your spine on the exhale. See if you can notice any shifts in your body. A shift might feel like a release of tension in your shoulders or a calm sensation in your stomach. Notice where you feel the shifts. Feel the sensation of air going in and out of your nose and the rise and fall of your belly. Allow your mind to wander and bring it back to the breath. Focusing on your breath will take practice.

Awareness and insight: Awareness and insight truly matter when we are able to link them to action. If I am aware that I am angry but still punch the wall or throw an object, that awareness has neither altered my mind-set nor my behavior. Mindfulness allows us to observe the emotion that leads to the negative behavior so that we can commit to avoiding the negative behavior and making a healthier choice instead, such as a deep breath, loving-kindness, or radical acceptance. Deep breath can change your mood and alter your mind-set. When a driver cuts you off, loving-kindness creates flexibility. I might think of sending gratitude to that person or consider that they might be having a bad day. Radical acceptance is nonjudgmental acknowledgment of a situation. For example, I might think, *There is traffic, I am sitting in it, and my emotion does not change the traffic pattern.* We can access all of these healthy behaviors when we engage with our awareness and insight.

Taking time to slow down: Making time to pause and slow down is something most of us struggle with in today's world. Have you ever just sat and done nothing? No phones, no reading material, no music or TV, no conversation, no daydreaming—just sitting. Many of us have not. Mindfulness creates space to do so, to commit to moments where we pause, perhaps to take a few breaths, watch the trees move in the wind, or observe the people around you. We also commit to slowing down—scheduling time for ourselves to do nothing rather than constantly socializing or working.

Connecting with values: Mindfulness practices enable us to prioritize what is important and to label these things as our values. Examining, assessing, and prioritizing values can encourage us to change a career or go back to school, assess the reciprocity of a relationship, or get involved in some community volunteer programs. You will have the chance to examine your values later in this chapter.

Chödrön wrote that the six *paramitas*, which is a Sanskrit word that translates to "perfections," provide a pathway to compassionate living, including generosity, discipline, patience, enthusiasm, meditation, and wisdom. Consider these practices, and your curiosity to learn more, the most critical building blocks. Your openness and curiosity to experience and learn will create your pathway to compassionate living.

Connection with the Self

I have found that many of us are afraid to connect on a deeper level to ourselves or others. Have you noticed that in yourself or someone close to you? Maybe you do not invite people into your home as often as you would like. Perhaps you always date people who are emotionally unavailable or unhealthy. You might eat or drink to excess a few times each week. Connection of any kind is challenging and, frankly, frightening. It makes us feel vulnerable, a term that Brené Brown defined as "uncertainty, risk, and emotional exposure." But there is much to be gained from moving through that vulnerability.

The practice of mindfulness involves vulnerability, and it can be scary at first. As we become more aware, slow down, and experience ourselves more fully, we might become alarmed. Those loud noises inside ourselves that we have been trying to avoid have just been turned up. We can hear them more clearly, in high definition. But if you continue to practice openness and nonjudgment, you will grow, and your relationship with yourself—as well as your relationships with others—will grow, too.

Many of the exercises in this book will lead you into new, uncharted territory. They may make you feel uncertain. You're taking a risk by trying them, and I ask that you approach each exercise with openness to the experience. Allow your emotions to surface.

Trying one exercise per day is a good pace. Remember, this is a marathon, not a sprint. You want to build your endurance slowly so that you do not burn out.

MAKING TIME

On the following schedule, write how much time you are willing to commit each day to reading this book and developing your mindfulness practice. If you know you have a big event or discrepancy in your schedule, do not list a mindfulness practice on that day. Make this schedule reasonable and attainable; one minute per day is enough for now. Start small and see if you can increase the time over the course of this book. (We will revisit this schedule in the middle of the book and then again at the end.)

	MINDFULNESS PRACTICE TIME
MONDAY	
TUESDAY	
WEDNESDAY	
THURSDAY	
FRIDAY	
SATURDAY	
SUNDAY	

BREATH AND EMOTIONS

Think about the six belly breaths you took earlier in this chapter in the attentional breathing section (page 20). On the diagram of the body, circle where you felt emotion during that exercise.

Now, practice the attentional breathing exercise again. Push your belly out on the inhale and bring your belly button to your spine on the exhale. See if you can notice any shifts in your body. A shift might feel like a release of tension in your shoulders or a calm sensation in your stomach. Notice where you feel the shifts. Feel the sensation of air going in and out of your nose and the rise and fall of your belly. Allow your mind to wander and bring it back to the breath.

It is not important whether the emotion became better or worse the second time you did this exercise; we just want to create nonjudgmental experience. Circle on the diagram where you felt emotion the second time. Remember this area of your body because you will focus on it in later chapters.

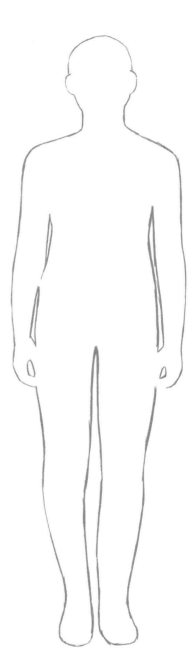

BREATH AND THOUGHTS

During the previous breathing exercise, what thoughts did you notice? In the following space, write down all the thoughts that came up. They could be negative, positive, or neutral. Practice nonjudgment and write down only the thoughts. Feel free to practice the breathing again; we can never practice enough deep breathing exercises.

LOVING-KINDNESS PART I

The following is a quote from Pema Chödrön about awareness and the practice of loving-kindness. On the following lines, copy the quote. Let it sink in and see what it means for you.

> *Holding on to beliefs limits our experience of life. That doesn't mean that beliefs or ideas or thinking is a problem; the stubborn attitude of having to have things be a particular way, grasping on to our beliefs and thoughts, all these cause the problems.*
>
> —Pema Chödrön

_____

_____

_____

_____

LOVING-KINDNESS PART II

Now, read the quote again and list three beliefs or ideas that you are holding on to:

1. _____

2. _____

3. _____

   The practice of loving-kindness is essential to beginning your mindfulness journey. We will dive deeper into that in chapter 6.

MINDFULNESS GOALS

Think about what lead you to pick up this book. You also have expectations for what you will have learned once you have finished this book. In this moment right now, what are your main goals and motivations for practicing mindfulness? The number of goals isn't important; you can have more than five or only one. Write down at least one goal for practicing mindfulness:

1. _____

2. _____

3. _____

4. _____

5. _____

PURPLE CUPCAKES

Defusion is the practice of realizing that the mind creates thoughts and emotions, but we are separate from those thoughts or emotions. To practice this technique, think of purple cupcakes.

   Sit in any comfortable seat, close your eyes, and imagine cupcakes with thick purple frosting. If you have a sweet tooth like I do, doing this might make you feel hungry or even salivate. Keep the image of purple cupcakes in your mind. Now, picture them falling from the ceiling or sky. You now have purple cupcakes all around you on the floor; you feel joy and hunger. Your eyes are still closed. Now, open your eyes and look around. Do you see any purple cupcakes? Practice this a few times.

WHAT ARE MY VALUES?

This worksheet can help you figure out what is important to you. In each column, mark how important you find that arena of your life. You might feel pulled to mark down what you think you *should* feel instead of what you actually feel. For example, you might feel like you have to mark family as a 9 because it is your cultural belief, even though you feel like it's actually more like a 5 in your own life. Instead, try to make your answers reflect where you actually are today and do your best to complete this nonjudgmentally. Values are fluid and will change over time, depending on what is important.

	NOT IMPORTANT									EXTREMELY IMPORTANT
ROMANTIC RELATIONSHIPS	0	1	2	3	4	5	6	7	8	9
FAMILY	0	1	2	3	4	5	6	7	8	9
PARENTING	0	1	2	3	4	5	6	7	8	9
FRIENDS AND SOCIALIZING	0	1	2	3	4	5	6	7	8	9
WORK	0	1	2	3	4	5	6	7	8	9
EDUCATION	0	1	2	3	4	5	6	7	8	9
RECREATION AND PHYSICAL ACTIVITY	0	1	2	3	4	5	6	7	8	9
COMMUNITY	0	1	2	3	4	5	6	7	8	9
SPIRITUALITY OR RELIGION	0	1	2	3	4	5	6	7	8	9
SELF-CARE	0	1	2	3	4	5	6	7	8	9

Remember this exercise. Later, we will look at values again and create an intention for actionable change.

SIX *PARAMITAS* (PERFECTIONS)

In the following circles, write at least one goal for each of the *paramitas*. Think of actions you can take to practice those *paramitas* in your life. For example, for "generosity," I could write that I will volunteer for two hours this month at the local food bank; for "meditation," I could write that I will commit to five minutes of meditation, two days per week. Try this for each circle. If you get stuck on one circle, move on to the next.

Generosity   Discipline   Patience

Enthusiasm   Meditation   Wisdom

COMPASSIONATE LIVING

Write down examples of ways you can show compassion. Many of the clients I have worked with are unsure of what this looks like. Here are some suggestions: smiling at a stranger on the street, bringing coffee for a coworker, sitting without distraction, and listening to a loved one in need.

Chapter 3

FOCUS ON THE PRESENT MOMENT

Within the context of mindfulness, pain and suffering are natural. This is a thought borrowed from Zen Buddhism. Pain is caused by holding on to something from the past, worrying about the future, having attachments, and having desire. The solution is to focus on the present moment instead. In this chapter, we will learn practices to remain in the present moment. We will also learn more about how, even though our brains are designed to judge, we can work toward nonjudgment.

PRESENT MOMENT AWARENESS

Today proceeds on through today.

—Dogen Zenji, translation by Michael Eido Luetchford

Many Buddhist teachings, including those from Japanese Buddhist Dogen Zenji, focus on the present moment. This is not an easy concept for beginners to mindfulness to grasp, especially after growing up in Western cultures that honor achievement and overworking. The quote from Dogen acknowledges the Zen Buddhist teaching that time moves from one present moment to the next present moment. There is no pain or suffering in the present moment because it has either already passed or not yet arrived. The goal as we build our practice in mindfulness is to describe and engage with the present moment.

Once, while I was driving to a training in the next state over, I was running late. Then, I hit traffic. Then, a thunderstorm hit. In the middle of it all, I noticed a vibrant red flower in the median. Its color was so bold that I was pulled to focus on that flower. In that moment, I accepted that I was in a storm, stuck in traffic, and late to the training. As I had recently begun learning about mindfulness and Zen Buddhism (in fact, that training was my first intensive training in dialectical behavioral therapy, a treatment that uses mindfulness as one of the core components), I realized how mindfulness works. I was still frustrated and annoyed that I was late. However, my practice of describing the flower in that present moment created space for the feelings and, eventually, for those feelings to decrease. That is an example of present moment awareness. The red flower was right there, and describing it brought me out of my frustrations and worries and into the present moment.

Present moment refers to the "here and now." I have found that this is one of the most challenging things for people to experience. So many people are focused on the next moment. For example, while traveling, there is an emphasis on where we are going. You board a plane, change the time zone on your watch to that of your destination, and do not focus on the flight, let alone on the feelings of anxiety that you may feel anyway while traveling on a plane. Rather, you are anxious to get to the destination. We create an illusion that once we arrive at some future place, things will be better or suffering will end. This takes us out of the present moment. The future actually exists nowhere other than in our thoughts, which is more philosophical than we will get in this book. But to highlight that in slightly simpler context, consider this quote by Eckhart Tolle: "Your entire life exists of this present moment."

The practice of mindfulness creates alignment with wherever you are and whatever you are doing in this moment. You might not want to be in that exact place. You might be experiencing something you wished you didn't have to (like surgery or being stuck in traffic), or you might be trying to escape your current feelings. As long as you take that next step into the next moment, that is present moment action. The focus within mindfulness practice is to engage with full attention to each step, without focusing on where you were or where you are going. Of course, this doesn't mean you shouldn't have a direction and a plan. We are encouraged to do that in the present moment. As goal-driven individuals, many feel they cannot be in the present moment because they are working toward some big goal. But the main practice is to mindfully develop your future plan in this moment.

Let's say that you want to finish college and get your bachelor's degree. You must develop a plan, which includes writing application essays, visiting and applying to schools, selecting a major, and so on. Present moment living provides you with the opportunity to map out a list of schools, write pro and con lists about various majors and the campuses, and feel worry and excitement about this step. If you were to focus only on graduating, there would be so much suffering, because this outcome is three to four years away. And once you graduate, then what? When I work with emerging adults, there is a constant theme of rushing to get where they are going. Have you ever experienced that? What happens once you arrive after rushing? You are likely focused on what you have to do next or annoyed about the fact that you had to rush to arrive there.

You might remember that we discussed present moment focus and nonjudgment in chapter 1. They are both relevant to this chapter, as well. We cannot experience the present moment fully without practicing nonjudgment.

Practice Nonjudgment

The brain is hardwired to judge. This means that neurologically, especially in the frontal lobe area, judgment is a natural process. We are meant to judge situations to figure out if they are safe or unsafe (think environment and danger), what we like and dislike (think food and personality types), and our aesthetic preferences (midcentury modern or rustic). The practice of mindfulness does not eliminate these judgments from our brain functioning; rather, we raise awareness to the judgments. When we acknowledge the judgments, we can remain in control rather than letting our judgments control us.

If you choose a career based on family pressure, marry someone who is not totally right for you but was right in other people's eyes, or buy a blue car even though you really wanted a red one, these are behavioral decisions that are the result of judgments. The practice of mindfulness teaches us to label judgments and work toward neutral judgments. You will recall this example from before: this is the best book ever (positive judgment); this is the worst book ever (negative); this is a book about mindfulness for beginners (neutral). We aim to get into that neutral judgment of our experiences.

Some people believe that if they get to a place of nonjudgment, or neutral judgment, they will no longer feel joy. But it is quite the opposite. As we develop the ability to shift to neutral judgments of situations, we experience them more fully. It is the same with good or bad emotions; nonjudgment does not mean that we can choose which emotions we feel or how often we feel them. Rather, we focus on describing emotions as they come and go instead of holding on to the good feelings or ignoring the bad emotions. Nonjudgmentally, we describe them and give them space. Then, we commit to our next step, knowing only the direction we are stepping in but not focusing on how that next step feels or whether it is the right or wrong step.

Notice how you felt this chapter. Write some notes in the margins about whether it all makes sense, you rolled your eyes, or you feel like you are reading another language. All of that is okay; this is a process. We will practice judgment labeling during one of our following exercises.

STORYTELLING

Write a very short story about a person or thing in the present moment. Here is an example:

When I was 12, my family adopted a friendly and loving dog named Allie. We share unconditional love. Each morning I wake up, and Allie is wagging her tail and waiting for me to let her out. When I kiss her good morning, I say to myself, "Thank you and good morning, Allie." When I am with her, I am reminded that she only knows how to be in the present moment; she is ready to go out, go to the bathroom, and then eat.

_____

_____

_____

_____

_____

_____

_____

_____

_____

_____

_____

_____

_____

_____

_____

BODY SCAN

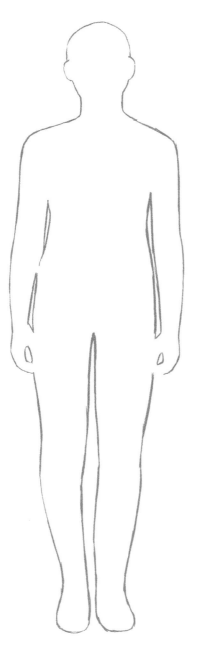

Body scans—a mental check-in with each part of your body—are useful for practicing many aspects of mindfulness. Here, we will use the body scan to be in the present moment.

While either seated or standing, take a deep breath and focus on your feet. Feel them on the floor. That is the present moment. Slowly shift your focus to one foot and work your way up one side of the body, stopping at each major part, before returning down the other side back to the feet.

Look at the illustration in this exercise if you're feeling confused about how body scans are supposed to work.

YOGA IN THE PRESENT MOMENT

Yoga is a practice of body movement that allows you to connect with the present moment nonjudgmentally. It is so easy to judge yourself against another yoga practitioner or the teacher. Take this moment to nonjudgmentally practice one of the poses pictured in this exercise. Remain in each pose for at least 30 seconds, but see how long you can hold the pose. See how long you can let go of judgment, too. The present moment practice is to focus on your pose only. As your mind drifts, bring it back to the pose and the breath.

I have selected four basic poses, but feel free to bring this into your own yoga practice, no matter your level.

PROS AND CONS OF JOURNALING

Another technique for connecting with the present moment is journaling. Let's first assess your readiness for journaling, which you can do in a notebook or electronically. In the following chart, write the pros and the cons for journaling. I included an example in the first line to help get you started:

PROS FOR JOURNALING	CONS FOR JOURNALING
I want to get the most out of this book, and Pete says it is beneficial.	I do not have the time.

If you find there are more pros than cons, then maybe you will consider starting to write in a journal this week. If there are more cons, let it go and move to the next exercise. The time is not right in this moment. That can and will change.

MANTRA

A mantra is a repeated phrase or rhythm that can aid concentration in meditation. When we repeat a saying, we are able to focus on just that saying. You can use your own prayer if you choose, but I have also included one for you here, along with check boxes to help you keep track of how many times you have repeated the mantra. This is sort of like mala beads in Buddhism or rosary beads in Catholicism, both of which help you keep track of how many times you've recited a prayer or mantra. There is no right number of times or length of time to repeat your mantra. Just sit and practice repeating the mantra. You can also write your own quote or mantra in the space provided here:

_____

_____

_____

_____

_____

_____

Mantra example: *Today proceeds on through today. I let go of the past and the future.*

Now, sit and repeat the mantra, either aloud or internally. Try for at least five minutes.

TIME IN THE PRESENT MOMENT

To practice understanding in the present moment, draw an analog clock with a minute hand and an hour hand. Then, draw the time that is currently on your clock or watch. Now, draw another clock next to it. Take a deep breath. Then, draw the current time in this moment.

Notice anything? By the time you have finished drawing the hands on the clock, the time has already changed. That is present moment awareness.

SOCIAL MEDIA GOALS

The use of mobile devices and social media really takes us out of the present moment. We have all spent time mindlessly scrolling and swiping at some point in our lives, and we can all work to cut down on our device usage. In the first column, list the top three to four apps that you use most on your device. In the second column, record the number of minutes/hours that you currently use the app each day. If you are unsure, write an estimate. (Screen time apps can help you figure out this number if you have no clue.) In the third column, write how much time you would like to spend on the app each day. This should be a decrease. Our overall intention here is to reduce the amount of time we spend using some applications on our device.

APPLICATION NAME	CURRENT USAGE	GOAL FOR USAGE

JUDGMENT

You will recall that our brains are hardwired to judge. Judgments themselves are not bad, but we want to ensure that we notice judgments in each moment. In the practice of mindfulness, we work toward neutral judgment so that we can nonjudgmentally experience the moment. Complete the following table to work toward neutral judgment. After looking at the word in the first column, write the first thing that comes to your mind in the second column. Then practice positive, negative, and neutral judgments.

WORD	FIRST THOUGHT	POSITIVE	NEGATIVE	NEUTRAL
BEACH (EXAMPLE)	Magical	Beautiful	Sand is uncomfortable	Beach has sand and ocean
MY MANAGER				
TREES				
MY FAMILY				
DOGS				
CATS				
PHYSICAL EXERCISE				
THE U.S.				
THE UNIVERSE				
HIKING				
MY BEST FRIEND				
CAKE AND COOKIES				
MEDICINE				
MEDITATION				

There is no right or wrong way to complete this exercise. You just want to practice raising your awareness to present-moment living and the natural way of judging.

MINDFUL WALKING

Dress for the weather. Leave devices at home or in your workplace. Step outside. With no task or goal, just walk. As you walk, pay attention and nonjudgmentally describe your feet on the ground, heel to toe. What do you hear? What do you see? Notice your thoughts. Allow them to come in and allow them to go out, like the clouds in the sky, each passing by. They're not holding on to the past or worrying about the future. They're just floating past the horizon. Do this for as long as you can. Try to begin with a minimum of five minutes and slowly build up your time each time you practice mindful walking.

BREAKING DOWN JUDGMENTS

I. Write at least two judgments you noticed today.
Example: Walking into the supermarket, I saw a fit person and sucked in my belly. I noticed judgment about the food that fit person eats, compared to what I eat.

_____

_____

_____

_____

II. What were these judgments related to?
Example: These judgments were related to my nutrition and my body image.

_____

_____

_____

_____

III. Is this judgment part of a pattern? If so, what is that pattern and how often do you experience it?

Example: I notice that when I walk into a store, I look at others, compare myself to them, and feel ugly. This happens almost every time I enter a store.

_____

_____

_____

_____

_____

IV. What have you learned from this?

Example: I can practice acceptance of my body, commit to healthier nutrition, and work on nonjudgment of others when I am in the store.

_____

_____

_____

_____

_____

JOURNAL JUDGMENTS

When it comes to noticing judgments, one technique that I find very effective is to simply write down judgments as they come up. You can do this in a notebook, in a notes file on your mobile device, or in the following space. Log your judgments from moment to moment, as they stand out, and keep notes. I have found it best to write them down as they occur. The more we write them down, the less we will experience them . . . but for now, just focus on writing them down. That is your task throughout the remainder of your work in this book.

Chapter 4

SET INTENTIONS

When we commit to action in a mindful manner, we do so with an intention. Intentions are when we plan actions that are aligned with values. They are voluntary and done with a heightened level of consciousness. Let's look at why and how we set intentions.

WHY SET AN INTENTION?

Intentions are somewhat abstract, like describing a color you have yet to see. We know they exist, and they can shape appearance and perception. Yet they are not necessarily part of the common language, and they are challenging to describe. When is the last time you were asked, "What was your intention when you went into work today?"

On a technical level, intentions are simply what one intends to do. Any action includes an intention, but mindfulness raises our awareness of these intentions. In mindfulness, intentions are conscious, tied to our values, and done with purpose. Our thoughts create goals. An intention is comprised of the thoughts that make up the plan that we need to achieve those goals.

In mindfulness, we aim to increase our own awareness within ourselves. As we become more aware, more conscious, we can hear the values inside us a little more clearly and are better able to consciously set intentions for our actions. This is why intentions often include an aspect of spirituality (or morality) to bring healing and peace to someone or something in need. These kinds of intentions might involve helping an elderly person cross the street, contacting a friend we know is suffering, sending a card to a lonely grandparent or relative, hiking to be in nature and exercise, or cleaning the dishes after dinner.

Intentions are not linear and are confounded by many variables, making them hard to study and even harder to comprehend in behavioral science. Being nonlinear means that they change; they go left and right, up and down. This is because many factors impact intentions. For example, I might have the intention to work out today, but then my child gets sick and I have to take her to the doctor. So, my intention of working out just changed. I may have to do it later when I get home from the doctor, or perhaps tomorrow.

Setting intentions requires awareness of thoughts that drive our behavior to the committed action. We do so through the mind, with a heightened consciousness and with some higher-level acknowledgment involving spirituality, religiosity, or morality.

What Does Setting Intentions Look Like?

Buddhist scholars have written extensively about the power of intentions and have incorporated them into meditations and lifestyle. In psychology, Lush and colleagues reported that mindfulness meditators had greater awareness of intentions, were more likely to acknowledge intentions, and were faster to notice judgment of the intention.

We can set intentions by writing them in a journal or on a sticky note on our bathroom mirror, scheduling a reminder, or telling a family member who will hold us accountable.

Intentions can be set for any value. (Recall the values inventory you took in chapter 2.) An intention related to the value of romantic relationships could be telling your partner "I love you" and complimenting one of their outfits this week. An intention related to the value of family could be studying with your child for 30 minutes, two nights this week. An intention related to the value of friendship could be committing to being a curious friend today and calling two friends you have not spoken to in some time, just to see how they are doing. An intention related to the value of work could be to put your phone on silent during work so that you can complete your task list faster than you did last week.

Though it might seem like intentions exist only in your mind, taking them out into the world can be a powerful mechanism for holding yourself accountable. Once we say an intention, it has been spoken into some reality. So, try to say them out loud. You may also write them down, create a reminder in your calendar, keep a journal, download an application for your device that might assist with intentions (e.g., an application called "Mindfulness"), or perform an arts and crafts exercise to create a vision board. (We will discuss vision boards in greater depth later.) You could even share your intentions with someone you trust to create an added layer of accountability. The louder the volume is, the more you may benefit from setting these intentions.

VALUES INFORM INTENTIONS

Rate your values to evaluate where you are likely to observe your greatest intentions. Those values that are most important to us in this moment are likely to have the most mindful intentions. You can look back at the values worksheet from chapter 2 (page 27) and compare, but attempt to complete this with a beginner's mind (page 9). If you complete it in this moment, once you are done, feel free to look back on your last values exercise and see if anything has changed.

	NOT IMPORTANT								EXTREMELY IMPORTANT
ROMANTIC RELATIONSHIPS	0	1	2	3	4	5	6	7	8	9
FAMILY	0	1	2	3	4	5	6	7	8	9
PARENTING	0	1	2	3	4	5	6	7	8	9
FRIENDS AND SOCIALIZING	0	1	2	3	4	5	6	7	8	9
WORK	0	1	2	3	4	5	6	7	8	9
EDUCATION	0	1	2	3	4	5	6	7	8	9
RECREATION AND PHYSICAL ACTIVITY	0	1	2	3	4	5	6	7	8	9
COMMUNITY	0	1	2	3	4	5	6	7	8	9
SPIRITUALITY OR RELIGION	0	1	2	3	4	5	6	7	8	9
SELF-CARE	0	1	2	3	4	5	6	7	8	9

SETTING INTENTIONS FOR YOUR VALUES

In the following section, write at least one intention for each of your primary values. Make sure that your intentions, which are similar to goals, are SMART (specific, measurable, achievable, relevant, and time limited). You don't want to set the intention, "I will have 15 million dollars in my bank account tomorrow." That is unlikely and unreasonable. You want to set an intention like, "I will complete 30 minutes of exercise three times this week," "I will complete my degree by the end of the year," or "I will host one family barbecue each month."

VALUE	INTENTION
ROMANTIC RELATIONSHIPS	
FAMILY	
PARENTING	
FRIENDS AND SOCIALIZING	
WORK	
EDUCATION	
RECREATION AND PHYSICAL ACTIVITY	
COMMUNITY	
SPIRITUALITY OR RELIGION	
SELF-CARE	

ENVIRONMENTAL INTENTION

Whether you are an environmentalist, a tree hugger, green, or still learning about it all, we can all appreciate the magnitude of Mother Nature.

In the following space, write one intention related to the environment.

Example: On my next trip to the beach, I will pick up garbage that others have left behind and throw it away in the proper receptacle.

_____

_____

_____

_____

_____

HEALTH INTENTION

I have never completed a physical exercise and thought, "Boy, I wish I had not done that." Exercise, at the right time and in the right amount, works for everyone. That is basic physiology. As we foster mindful living, this will include mindfulness of action and movement. In the following space, write one intention about your health.

Example: I intend to eliminate processed sugar from my diet every Monday and Friday for the month of April.

_____

_____

_____

_____

_____

WHAT DOES IT MEAN TO YOU?

Intentions compressed into words enfold magical power. —Deepak Chopra

What does this quote mean to you?

_____

_____

_____

_____

_____

_____

_____

_____

_____

_____

_____

_____

_____

_____

_____

_____

INTENTIONS FOR THE WEEK

In the following calendar, write at least one small intention for each day, with the goal of practicing daily mindful intentions. An intention could be as simple as finishing a home project or an assignment, but also think about incorporating your values from the previous exercises. For example, for the value of spirituality/religion, I could make an intention to learn more about a belief system I do not know much about (e.g., Islam or Judaism).

DAYS	INTENTIONS
MONDAY	
TUESDAY	
WEDNESDAY	
THURSDAY	
FRIDAY	
SATURDAY	
SUNDAY	

INTENTION CARDS

Write cards to two people in your life who have had an impact on you, good or bad. On that card, set an intention for them. Even if the person has had a negative impact on you, set an intention for their health or well-being to allow for your own healing. You do not have to send these cards; it's your choice.

Example 1: To someone who hurt me.
Dear Carl,
I notice and accept that you are still managing your suffering. It hurt when you took advantage of me, my home, and my resources. I am stronger for it today. Today, I intend to send you healing and peaceful energy. Hoping you find peace.

Example 2: To someone very close to me.

Dear Mom,

Children don't come with instruction manuals, and while you were not perfect, I am so thankful for all you have done. I set the intention to call you twice per week so that I can hear your voice, smile when frustrated, and celebrate your being and your rearing me.

CELEBRATING INTENTIONS

Have you become slightly more aware of your intentions since reading chapter 4? Write down five intentions that you are now more aware of. You may have realized that you have been living with intentions about your health, parent, loved one, career, etc. Share those intentions here and bring them to a higher level of consciousness by writing them down.

1. _____

2. _____

3. _____

4. _____

5. _____

VISION BOARD

When was the last time you completed an arts and crafts project? As we age, we live life with a level of seriousness and responsibility that makes us forget some of the enjoyments of life. A vision board is both an enjoyable arts and crafts project and a way to help focus on intentions.

A vision board is a piece of paper or cardboard that you fill with images or words related to your goals and aspirations. This board will encompass your intentions for life in this moment. If you've never made a vision board before, here are some simple instructions:

1. Grab some old magazines or newspapers, plus scissors, glue or tape, and a piece of paper, cardboard, or poster paper.

2. Think about what things are important to you, your values, and your committed intentions.

3. Search through the magazines or newspapers for words or images that embody those values and intentions. For example, if you want to swim once per week and you see an ad where someone is swimming, you can cut that out and place that on the board.

4. Continue until you fill out the board.

5. Post this board somewhere you will see it daily, like the closet, bathroom, or garage.

YOGIC INTENTION

What is the first thing that dogs do when they wake up? They stretch, as do most other animals. What do we do? We are likely rushing to get where we are going that day. What if you set an intention, for the health of your mind and body, to stretch or practice some yoga poses at various times this week? Commit to doing some of the following poses every morning. What is your intention about those poses? Write them down here.

_____ _____ _____ _____

_____ _____ _____ _____

_____ _____ _____ _____

_____ _____ _____ _____

_____ _____ _____ _____

RELEASING NEGATIVITY

As we practice mindfulness, we learn that the present moment is enjoyable and we create peace. We also become more aware when we are holding on to negativity, and maybe we even see that it is holding us back.

Write down the top five negative experiences that you are holding on to.

Example: Former business partner stole money from me and the company.

1. _____

2. _____

3. _____

4. _____

5. _____

Now, next to each experience, write an intention to release the negativity tied to that experience.

Example: I release the experience with my business partner. I have a new job and I have peace.

Chapter 5

SPEND TIME WITH YOUR THOUGHTS AND FEELINGS

While we are alive (and perhaps afterwards, too), we think and we feel. As far as we know, there is no way to stop thoughts or feelings, so we must find a way to live with them. The practice of mindfulness builds a relationship with our thoughts and feelings, teaching us about the role of thoughts and their relationship to our feelings. This chapter will focus on fostering a relationship with your thoughts and understanding your feelings.

BECOME AN OBSERVER

Observing means focusing on internal and external stimuli, such as thoughts, emotions, and physical sensations (i.e., bodily experiences), as well as our physical environment. Psychologists, especially cognitive behavioral therapy (CBT) specialists, look at ways in which thoughts become distorted, or do not match up with reality. In 1989, psychiatrist David Burns published a list of the most common cognitive distortions that people experience.

Cognitive Distortions

These are basic examples with simplified definitions. See the Resources section (page 161) for a more in-depth look at each of these cognitive distortions.

1. **All-or-nothing thinking:** Seeing things as good or bad, black or white, with no in-between. Example: I either work out every day for two hours, or not at all.

2. **Overgeneralization:** One bad event means that you are stuck in a constantly defeated life pattern. Example: I sprained my ankle and think that means that I always hurt myself.

3. **Mental filter:** One small event changes the entire situation. Examples: I broke a nail, so my entire outfit is ruined; I argued with my partner, so our vacation is ruined.

4. **Disqualifying the positive:** Disregarding positive events in your life. Example: I got a raise, but I don't deserve it because I am not even working as hard as I could.

5. **Jumping to conclusions (mind reading or fortune telling):** You think you already know how someone will respond to you. Example: There's no point in following up with Susan about that job lead. I know she only mentioned it to be nice.

6. **Catastrophizing or minimization:** Making mountains out of molehills or downplaying serious situations. Example: I just broke my finger, but it's not a big deal. I'll go deal with it once my friend's big graduation luncheon is over.

7. **Emotional reasoning:** Believing emotions wholeheartedly. Example: I feel anxious, so I must be in danger.

8. **"Should" statements:** Thoughts and intentions based on values, but often not your own values. Example: I should be married. I should have a better job. I should volunteer at the library, even though I don't like to read very much.

9. **Labeling or mislabeling:** Similar to overgeneralization but more intense. Example: I stubbed my toe, and that means that I am a terrible and unco-ordinated human being.

10. **Personalization:** You blame yourself for all things that go wrong. Example: He stopped talking to me, so I must have said the wrong thing.

One of the most common distortions is emotional reasoning. This means we believe what we feel, even if it is not logical: "I feel something, therefore it must be real." When I step onto a crowded train, I might start to feel tightness in my chest, become sweaty, and notice thoughts like "How do I get out?" or "What if we need to evacuate fast?" The interaction between those physical sensations (tight chest, fast breathing, sweating) and thoughts ("How do I get out?"), create the behavior of wanting to escape. Hence, those feelings of anxiety and negative thoughts make me believe there is danger and it is real. However, trains move all along the globe, full and empty, and arrive at their destination with no issue. There is not necessarily a factual basis for my feelings in that moment.

Let's try another example. Michael has one sister, Lisa, and they get along well. As their parents age and become more dependent, they begin to discuss extended care. Michael and Lisa have seen eye-to-eye all along. Recently, though, Lisa's husband has alluded to his belief that he and Lisa should be the executors for her parents because they are more stable, have a family, and can more easily manage stress. Michael feels enraged by this. He starts to pace, begins sweating, and goes over in his mind how he is going to show up at his sister's house, fight with her, and change her mind. He notices thoughts like "They think I am dumb" and "They think I don't have money management skills." None of those thoughts are factual, but because he feels angry, Michael begins to believe them. He runs a large company and has a graduate degree, but he is single and childless, which has created feelings of vulnerability and aggravated a sore spot. When our insecurities come out, many of us act out.

With mindfulness, we practice observing our thoughts and feelings. In the train example, we would observe the thoughts about the train and practice separating from them. Sometimes I can picture the thoughts as clouds passing in the sky, leaves floating down a river, or cars racing around a racetrack. Sometimes the thoughts come back, but with practice, they will come back less often and with less force. When people describe having panic attacks, there is almost always an attachment to those thoughts as factual, and the person cannot see differently.

Becoming an observer would let Michael defuse from the thoughts that he is "dumb" or that he doesn't "have money management skills." When he felt anger, these thoughts became facts. With the practice of mindfulness, Michael could take a few deep breaths, watch these thoughts, and practice observing the mind. Once his feelings have settled, he might be able to see that his sister has two children, both of whom are adults and professionals, who could also assist with their parents while they age. Of course, this is just one perspective, but the key is to highlight the distortion.

Some parts of CBT research encourage people to stop thoughts or to change them: If you have a negative thought that you are ugly, stop it and change it to a positive thought. When I hear this, I think of the 1986 film *Back to School* with Rodney Dangerfield, where he is attending a self-improvement workshop and is asked to repeat, "I am loved. I am beautiful," while looking in a mirror. That would be great if it worked. However, it is not reasonable. We all have so many negative thoughts and don't walk around believing them all of the time. No matter how positive we are, there will still be negative thoughts and second-guessing. Some research suggests that at least two-thirds of thoughts are negative. That is part of the hardwiring of human brains. Stopping thoughts might work for some people. The rest of us can practice acceptance and observance of the thoughts and feelings.

The goal in mindfulness is to build a relationship with thoughts and a practice of acceptance of thoughts and subsequent feelings. Thoughts and feelings are linked, but in mindfulness, we do not try to change them. We learn to exist with our thoughts and feelings.

Another drawback of engaging too much with your thoughts and feelings is that it can become mentally and emotionally exhausting. It's almost like becoming the ball in a tennis match, instead of being a fan in the audience. The ball goes back and forth, back and forth. On the other hand, fans are moving their heads back and forth to watch the tennis ball, which is better than being the ball that is hit back and forth. Better yet, some fans in the stand are able to watch with full perception, which means their head remains at the net and their eyes can follow the ball. They can stay relaxed and see the entire court for what it is and what is happening on it, which is much less taxing. The fans watch the center court and ball without moving their neck muscles. Similarly, we can watch and observe our own thoughts and emotions and stay much more aware of the entire situation.

Research published in the *American Journal of Nursing Research* points to positive effects of becoming an observer of thoughts and feelings through mindfulness, including reduced stress, anxiety, and depression.

Accept and Let Go

Observing leads to acceptance, which ultimately leads to being able to let go. Acceptance is being able to nonjudgmentally describe a situation without holding on to it, and letting it go since it is in the past and there is nothing we can do about it. Have you ever just watched clouds passing in the sky? They are not worried about leaving you or where they are going. They are just perfectly and graciously passing by. As we practice observing, we learn nonattachment and practice letting go. We are not our thoughts, we are not our feelings, and we are not factually bound to how our body feels.

In the example of Michael and Lisa trying to decide who will be the executor of their parents' wills, Michael is able to let go and have dinner with his sister and brother-in-law later that night. He recognized his thoughts and feelings (body sensations and pacing), he accepted their role in his behavior, and then he was able to let go and enjoy dinner.

Many clients feel stuck with acceptance. I believe that this is one of the most challenging aspects of mindful living. I suspect this is because we live in a world that is focused on winning and being right, which prevents us from accepting where we are and letting go. Many people, as in the case of Michael, would try to get back at their sister and brother-in-law. Many would fight to remain the executor rather than understanding why it makes sense to allow their sister and brother-in-law to take the reins. As we have learned, mindfulness can change the brain. Those changes in the brain make acceptance and letting go easier. The more we practice mindfulness, the stronger our "brain muscles" become, allowing us to more easily accept and let go.

MAKING MORE TIME

Let's check in to see how you have been doing with your scheduling. On the following schedule, write how much time you are able to commit each day for your mindfulness practice and reading this book. Remember, if you know you have a big event or discrepancy in your schedule, do not list a mindfulness practice or reading on that day. Make sure to make this schedule reasonable and attainable, but also remember to keep pushing yourself. By this point, you could have increased your practice time to between 5 and 15 minutes per day. Remember, we are building muscle.

WEEK 1 MINDFULNESS PRACTICE TIME	
MONDAY	
TUESDAY	
WEDNESDAY	
THURSDAY	
FRIDAY	
SATURDAY	
SUNDAY	

WEEK 2 MINDFULNESS PRACTICE TIME	
MONDAY	
TUESDAY	
WEDNESDAY	
THURSDAY	
FRIDAY	
SATURDAY	
SUNDAY	

OBSERVING DISTORTIONS

Many of our thoughts are distorted, meaning there could be some factual basis to them, but they are also often inaccurate. Being able to separate from them and label them allows us to manage how we respond to our thoughts more effectively. The following table shows the cognitive distortions from pages 62–63. Refer back to that chart for descriptions of each.

When you notice a strong emotion over the next two weeks, find and label the thought that accompanies it. Write down which category of cognitive distortion it belongs to in a notebook or on your phone. After the two weeks end, note on the following chart how often you had each cognitive distortion, and write an example of each kind of distortion that will help you identify it in the future. Make note of the top three or four cognitive distortions you experience; those are important to be aware of.

COGNITIVE DISTORTION	EXAMPLE	HOW OFTEN?
ALL-OR-NOTHING THINKING		
OVERGENERALIZATION		
MENTAL FILTER		
DISQUALIFYING THE POSITIVE		
JUMPING TO CONCLUSIONS		
CATASTROPHIZING OR MINIMIZATION		
EMOTIONAL REASONING		
"SHOULD" STATEMENTS		
LABELING OR MISLABELING		
PERSONALIZATION		

PLACING THOUGHTS ON CLOUDS

Consider one of your favorite outdoor spaces on a partly cloudy day. Next, think about a feeling or thought that you have been dealing with. On the lines provided within the clouds, write down what you are attempting to release. When you go outside later, perhaps you can look up, describe some clouds, and imagine these words on those clouds as they pass by.

HOW TO NOT THINK A THOUGHT

Is there a thought that keeps nagging at you? A thought that has been hard to let go and to accept? For example, you might notice thoughts that are critical of your body: *I'm fat; I'm ugly; my calves are too skinny.* Or perhaps there's something about your personality someone recently commented on negatively: *I'm lazy and disorganized; I'm a workaholic.* In this exercise, we are going to work on suppressing this thought. As a warning, you will probably find that you are unable to suppress it.

1. Write the problem or thought that has been nagging you.

_____

_____

_____

_____

_____

2. Now, spend five minutes trying to suppress the thought. Push it away. Try your best not to think about that thought.

3. How many times did that thought cross your mind during those five minutes?

_____

_____

_____

_____

4. Now, invite that thought back in and spend the same time with it, also about five minutes. But this time, also do something active that comes naturally. Take a walk, pet your dog, or draw a picture.

5. Now, how many times did that thought cross your mind?

_____

_____

_____

_____

_____

_____

What have we learned? We cannot suppress thoughts. No matter how hard we try, thoughts will arise. The goal in the practice of mindfulness is to acknowledge the thought, accept it, and then practice letting it go. When we engage in activities that are in the present moment, we notice that we are less nagged by the thoughts we are trying to push away.

RADICAL ACCEPTANCE

When we enter the highway and see traffic, we cannot change being stuck in traffic. No matter how hard we hit the steering wheel or how frustrated we become, we are still in traffic. One key aspect to *radical acceptance* is nonjudgment.

In the following area, draw your favorite object. It could be a flower, a house, a car, or stick figures. The goal is not to create a masterpiece. Just let yourself draw. Get as creative as you like and have fun!

Now, write down some thoughts about your drawing. Be sure to include your judgments about your artwork or this exercise more generally (e.g., "I forgot I am a good artist"; "Wow, I am terrible"; or "This exercise is silly"). After you are done writing, take one more glance at your artwork before moving on to the exercise "Acceptance and Letting Go." This is where we will see radical acceptance in action.

_____

_____

_____

_____

_____

_____

_____

_____

_____

_____

_____

_____

_____

_____

ACCEPTANCE AND LETTING GO

Let's build on what it means to practice nonattachment within mindfulness. Go back to your drawing from the exercise "Radical Acceptance" and scribble all through it. Make it look different. Erase parts of it and even mess it up completely if you feel like it. This is the practice of radical acceptance and letting go.

Now, accept that the image you just created is gone. As you watch your thoughts while you change the drawing, notice if you are resistant to changing it, wishing to hold on to it, thinking about moving to the next exercise, or just thinking about a fight you had earlier today. This practice is a reminder of the impermanence of everything. No matter how lovely an object is, everything can and does change. The practice of acceptance and letting go is at the core of practicing mindfulness.

EMOTIONAL INTELLIGENCE

Daniel Goleman has written about emotional intelligence (EI), which is basically a healthy relationship with one's feelings, including awareness of them. EI also helps us understand what triggers we experience for certain emotions, which helps us more easily label our emotions, and ultimately enables us to drive our emotions rather than let our emotions drive us. Sounds like mindfulness, right?

In the following chart, notice the variation of feelings. You can underline feelings that you have right now and then circle ones that you have not really experienced or are words that you do not typically use. You can photocopy this page or take a picture for your mobile device and then reference it throughout the weeks. Most adults do not have an expansive vocabulary related to their emotions. Use this exercise to begin growing your emotional vocabulary.

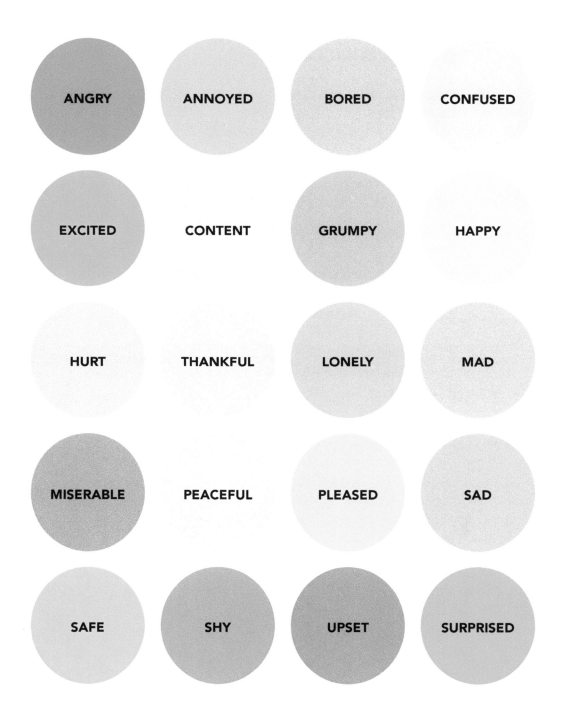

ANGRY   ANNOYED   BORED   CONFUSED

EXCITED   CONTENT   GRUMPY   HAPPY

HURT   THANKFUL   LONELY   MAD

MISERABLE   PEACEFUL   PLEASED   SAD

SAFE   SHY   UPSET   SURPRISED

BUILDING BRAIN MUSCLES

The brain is an organ that can change over time with brain plasticity. I have used the term "brain muscles" so that we can imagine that as we practice mindfulness, we are *building muscles* in our brain. Much of the research around meditation highlights that it is one of the most effective techniques to build these brain muscles. Meditation is not easy at first, and your relationship with it will ebb and flow, but with commitment it becomes a habit. Please consider committing to meditation; practice patience and just find what works for you. Here are a few ways that you can practice meditation:

1. Find an application on your phone with guided meditations (e.g., Calm or Headspace).

2. Use YouTube to find a guided meditation or instructions on how to meditate.

3. Listen to music that has no words (e.g., classical, jazz, or "liquid mind"), and sit in an upright posture.

4. Sit in the lotus position, hands in prayer, and observe your thoughts in silence.

The goal is to find something that works for you where you are still, observing, breathing, and just being.

DO NOTHING, JUST LISTEN

Practicing acceptance involves giving ourselves space while not engaging with the issue. Think of a time or an event when someone called you something negative. Maybe a manager at work criticized your performance or a coworker dismissed a project you were working on.

What were you called?

_____

_____

_____

Write the word here again in capital letters:

_____

_____

_____

Just sit and watch. Create space not to engage. Watch it over time, perhaps about five minutes, and see if the feelings disappear or decrease.

The practice of nonengagement with these kinds of insults builds strength in our mindfulness practice and allows for us to eliminate the need to win. We do not allow people to take advantage of us, and we also do not let others' insults have any impact on our own being.

BLACK IT OUT

As we continue to grow and build strength in these practices, let's throw out negativity based on past experiences. In the garbage can at right, write the negative things that you wish to throw away, the negative thoughts or events that you have been holding on to.

Then, scribble everything out until you can't see the words.

We are working toward releasing that which is no longer serving us. Throw it away. The more we practice this, the easier it becomes.

Generosity is the most natural outward expression of an inner attitude of compassion and loving-kindness.

—14th Dalai Lama

PART 2

CULTIVATING JOY, KINDNESS, CALM, AND MORE

By now, you have a sense of what the practice of mindfulness entails. You might be wavering between commitment and uncertainty, but hopefully you are curious about whether the practice will work. As you integrate the practice of mindfulness into your life, you begin to see benefits, such as increased joy and calmness and feeling kinder toward yourself and others. Part 2 will focus on how to cultivate these results.

Chapter 6

FIND KINDNESS, COMPASSION, AND EMPATHY

You may never become the next Buddha or the new Mother Teresa, but that doesn't mean that your smaller acts of kindness don't count. What about telling the waiter they did a good job, smiling and thanking the person at the grocery store checkout, or helping a stranger with directions? As we live and practice mindfulness, we are more aware of how we interact with our environment and become committed to making it a better place.

KINDNESS AND COMPASSION FOR YOURSELF AND OTHERS

As we work on cultivating kindness and compassion for ourselves and others in this chapter, I want to share a Buddhist saying often referenced in mindfulness and yoga called the Four Immeasurables. The Four Immeasurables has been shown to create health and well-being, along with other benefits, among those who recite it regularly. It reminds us that we all suffer together, that we seek compassion for those who are suffering, that we can find happiness together, and that we strive to gain peace by releasing attachment and negative emotions.

THE FOUR IMMEASURABLES

May all beings have happiness and the causes of happiness.

May all beings be free from suffering and the causes of suffering.

May all beings rejoice in the well-being of others.

May all beings live in peace, free from greed and hatred.

Empathy is the ability to observe another's pain and attempt to walk in their shoes. Compassion is the expression of empathy with boundaries, meaning that we do not take on another's pain when we express compassion. Compassion is embedded within the practice of mindfulness and shows up in many other philosophies and techniques, too; for instance, there has recently been a tremendous shift in psychology toward embracing behavioral concepts such as compassion with clients. However, compassion itself is not part of any one type of therapy, medical intervention, philosophy, or manualized treatment. You will find aspects of compassion and mindfulness present in a variety of therapies, such as Compassion Focused Therapy, Dialectical Behavioral Therapy, and Buddhist Psychology. There is evidence that the practice of compassion decreases depression and anxiety, creates a more enriching life, and fosters feelings of happiness and joy. To better understand the effects of compassion, it will be helpful to understand its basis and how it integrates with psychology.

The practice of compassion, which has been around since the beginning of human history, is standard in communities practicing Buddhism. Buddhism, the philosophy that accepts suffering as natural, practices releasing attachment and commits to that Eightfold Path (page 8). A number of mindfulness-based strategies reference Buddhist philosophy, and many Western practitioners of psychology, including Paul Gilbert and Marsha Linehan, have directly borrowed from the 3,000-year-old philosophy. Compassion Focused Therapy (CFT) is comprised of concepts you have read thus far, as it is a standard practice within mindfulness. Paul Gilbert said that the practice of CFT incorporates developmental aspects of psychology, evolutionary psychology, social psychology, neuroscience, and Buddhism.

Compassion is free. As is also the case with mindfulness, we do not need any memberships or fancy equipment to practice compassion. It simply requires that you pay attention to yourself and your environment, notice moments to share appreciation, remain mindful, and *show empathy while maintaining boundaries*. The boundaries are key.

The phrase "empathy with boundaries" might be confusing for some, so I want to break it down a bit. If you have ever flown on a commercial airplane, you have heard the pre-flight safety procedures in which they ask that you put on your own oxygen mask before helping a child or loved one with theirs. Why? Because if you lose consciousness while trying to help that child or loved one, you will not be able to help them at all. This is also the case with the practice of compassion. Showing empathy with boundaries is critical to remaining healthy and available for others. Charles R. Figley stated that if you show too much of it without boundaries, then you will feel exhausted and experience what is called *compassion fatigue*. If I were 100% compassionate 100% of the time, there would be nothing left. So, we must first practice compassion for ourselves.

Compassion for ourselves, or self-compassion, is the practice of allowing ourselves to be imperfect. This can be a very difficult thing to do because the mind possesses many negative thoughts and we are often self-critical. The brain uses more sensory encoding when negative events occur than when positive events occur, which is why you might be able to recall a bad memory more easily and with more detail than a good one. We focus on the things we have done poorly rather than recalling those things that we have done well. But the practice of self-compassion reminds us to celebrate all victories, no matter how large or how small.

Self-compassion is not something small that might slightly improve the quality of your life. It is massively important and can even be used to treat severe cases of PTSD, such as those suffered by 20% of U.S. military veterans. There is evidence that individuals with PTSD will recall the traumatic events more clearly than positive events, as the brain is wired to do. The practice of compassion can help untangle those neurological networks.

In one 2015 study, researchers found that the practice of self-compassion had a positive effect on PTSD symptoms. Specifically, they found that practices of self-compassion helped improve PTSD symptoms such as anxiety and sleep disturbances. The practice of self-kindness and mindfulness improved, and there were decreases in self-judgment, isolation, and overidentification with the trauma. Compassion has also been shown by Deborah A. Lee and Sophie James to be helpful in overcoming flashbacks and decreasing other common symptoms such as shame, guilt, and fear.

But compassion doesn't end with us. There's also compassion for others, which allows us to learn from people, listen with empathy, give to a cause or community, practice acceptance, and show kindness. In a basic sense, compassion for others is allowing a driver to go ahead of you, leaving an extra dollar tip, volunteering for a local organization, or asking someone you do not agree with some open-ended questions with real curiosity. People who practice compassion with others report higher positive mental states.

Loving-Kindness

Loving-kindness is a feeling experienced through the practice of mindfulness. Sharon Salzberg, a Buddhist practitioner and scholar, defined loving-kindness as "a form of inclusiveness of caring, rather than categorizing others in terms of those whom we care for and those who can be easily excluded, ignored or disdained." It is the ability to love yourself for all of your strengths and imperfections and truly accept things as they are. It creates a warming sensation around the heart area. In the practice of mindfulness, we are pulled to see how connected we are, and that is what we do with loving-kindness.

As a behavior, loving-kindness is demonstrating care for others and their well-being. Loving-kindness is also integral in the Mindfulness-Based Stress Reduction (MBSR) protocols as a foundational component; participants practice loving-kindness throughout the program. Some examples include listening to guided meditations related to forgiveness, writing down reflections on change in our lives, and accepting how fragile and precious life is.

SELF-COMPASSION

Everyone can benefit from practicing self-compassion at difficult times. Find a comfortable seat and imagine something that you have recently struggled with. Close your eyes. With your eyes closed and those feelings close to you, make strong fists and extend your arms out in front of you (palms down, closed fists). Really allow those feelings space and think of the event and associated emotions. Squeeze a little harder. Then, as you open your palms, rotate your hands toward the ceiling or sky. Imagine that those feelings or experiences float up, out of your hands, toward the ceiling or sky. Picture them getting further and further away and then open your arms out to the side. This creates an opening in your heart, an openness to a new experience, and allows you to feel as though you are about to take flight. Think of a bird's wings and opening your arm span. Then, cross your hands over your shoulders, giving yourself a strong and tight hug. Thank yourself for having the bravery to experience those emotions and for embracing the compassion that is necessary for this practice. Slowly and gently allow your hands to fall into your lap, keep your eyes closed, and take three deep breaths.

COMPASSION QUIZ

I am hard on myself when I make a mistake.	True	False
I judge others on how they behave.	True	False
I am judgmental of my own flaws.	True	False
When I fail, I accept it and move on easily.	True	False
I accept my flaws all the time.	True	False
When things are bad, I accept that as natural.	True	False

If you answered "true" to one or more items in the first three statements and "false" to one or more items in the second three statements, you will benefit from practicing more self-compassion. There is a free self-compassion quiz on the Resources list by Dr. Kristin Neff (page 161).

COMPASSION FOR A FRIEND

On the following lines, describe a situation where a friend or someone close to you was hurting and going through something really tough.

_____

_____

_____

_____

Now, what did you tell this friend? Write the advice you gave, things you said, and behaviors you practiced for this friend.

_____

_____

_____

_____

How did you feel when you helped this friend?

_____

_____

_____

Now, think of something you have struggled with recently.

_____

_____

_____

What did you tell yourself? What do you notice your mind telling you to do?

_____

_____

_____

How did you feel going through this challenge you just wrote about?

_____

_____

_____

Do you notice any differences about what you told your friend compared to what you told yourself? If so, write about that difference here:

_____

_____

_____

Often, we are better advice givers than practitioners, especially when it comes to ourselves. I suspect there are many examples where you would manage your friend's difficulties more effectively than your own. But compassion for the self as well as others will make us feel more joy and peace.

WRITE A LETTER

I often ask clients to write a letter to someone they are struggling with or to themselves. It might feel strange, but it is such a useful tool. Write a letter to this person and tell them how you feel about something you may have been holding on to, or something you have watched them struggle with. Just write what comes to mind and what you wish to share.

Here are some basic rules for writing the letter.

1. This letter is just for this exercise and is not meant to be shared with the person you're writing to.

2. Write the letter nonjudgmentally, as if no one will ever see it.

3. Be as close to 100% honest as possible while writing.

4. When you are done, read it aloud (or maybe read it to someone you trust).

LABELING SELF-CRITICISM

Over the next week, write down the adjectives that you notice pop into your mind when you are completing a task, such as while you are working out, driving, having a conversation with someone you admire, addressing a difficult conversation with someone you love, or brushing your teeth and looking in the mirror. Write descriptive words related to yourself in those situations. You can log them here, but you can also log them in a notebook, a journal, or an application on your phone.

BRAVING: COMPASSION AND TRUST IN OTHERS

Part of the practice of compassion is learning about who you can share your intimate struggles with. Go through each of the letters in Brené Brown's BRAVING acronym, which lists the seven elements of trust, and complete each section, fully thinking about how trustworthy your relationship with a loved one (or yourself) is.

Boundaries. In what ways has this person respected my boundaries in the past? In what ways have they not respected my boundaries? Does this person tend to express their own boundaries? Are they willing to say "No" when they need to?

_____

_____

_____

_____

Reliability. Does this person do what they say they will? Do they seem to be aware of their own ability to listen in a supportive way and when they might not be able to do that?

_____

_____

_____

_____

Accountability. When this person makes mistakes, do they own up and apologize?

_____

_____

_____

Vault. Does this person keep things that are told to them in confidence private (i.e., "keep it in the vault")?

_____

_____

_____

Integrity. Does this person tend to prioritize doing the right thing? Would they rather listen to someone who is having a hard time and be willing to feel discomfort, or are they more likely to choose their own comfort?

_____

_____

_____

Nonjudgment. Does this person tend to listen to others without expressing judgment? Do they talk to others in a way that shows that they find them to be acceptable or lovable just as they are?

_____

_____

_____

Generosity. Does this person tend to give people the benefit of the doubt and interpret their intentions and actions with great generosity?

_____

_____

_____

COMPASSION BRAINSTORM

After reading this chapter, did you think of any examples of how you might show compassion for others? This could include a friend, a family member, a coworker, a neighbor, or the local postal worker. Could you spend time with a friend doing their favorite activity? Could you make dessert for a family member?

Think hard about people you interact with, regularly or irregularly, whom you have not yet thought about or practiced with during these exercises.

In the following section, write down 10 ways that you can practice compassion for others (considering some of the people you might not have thought of the first time around):

_____

_____

_____

_____

_____

_____

_____

_____

_____

_____

_____

_____

_____

_____

_____

LOVE AND KINDNESS

With whom do you practice love and kindness most regularly? Write as many names as you can think of here:

- _____
- _____
- _____
- _____
- _____
- _____
- _____

Who shows you love and kindness most regularly? Write as many names as you can think of here:

- _____
- _____
- _____
- _____
- _____
- _____
- _____

How does it feel when you practice love and kindness and when you receive it? Are they any different? Reflect on the role of loving-kindness in your life at this point. When can you create more of it? When can you remember to enjoy it where it already exists?

THE POWER OF A SMILE

When I used to coach swimming, there were some athletes who walked around with their shoulders shrugged and a grim look on their face. They were not mad in that moment necessarily. They just had this kind of disposition. I would encourage them to stand upright, stick their chest out, and smile. Try it right now. Sit up or stand up straight. Smile.

What did you notice after you smiled?

_____

_____

_____

_____

_____

_____

_____

_____

_____

_____

The act of smiling makes our brains release happy hormones, such as oxytocin, so the more we smile, the better we feel. Sometimes, when I feel really stressed, I get up from my desk, take a small walk down the hallway or outside, and focus on smiling. It might look slightly odd, but I will feel much better afterwards, so who cares!

LOVING-KINDNESS MANTRAS

Choose one of the following phrases and write it at least three times:

I am loved and I have purpose.

I choose joy in the moment.

I let go of expectations.

You can also choose your own mantra or quote and write it in this same section.

_____

_____

_____

_____

_____

_____

_____

_____

_____

_____

_____

_____

_____

_____

Practice repeating the act and curiosity of love and kindness.

Chapter 7

RELAX AND FIND PEACE

Remember back in chapter 2 when I asked you whether you turn music on as soon as you get home or get in the car? Have you noticed more when you do it since reading that chapter? Have you perhaps even done it less often? The goal of mindfulness is to slow down and relax, which in turn will provide us with the opportunities to release stress and improve the quality of our lives. The more we become comfortable with quiet time, the less affected we are by the noise of our minds, and the healthier we become.

IT'S IMPORTANT TO SLOW DOWN

Mindfulness teaches us that we do not always have to be scheduled, completing a task, or socializing. It is acceptable to do nothing and to slow down.

Sally came to treatment because she had obsessive thoughts, worried about germs, and had challenges with romantic relationships. She also constantly felt tired. She was part of a large Latinx family, where she had nice relationships with everyone, and her parents were still together. She was hardworking and had a good support system with her friends, but she still felt something was wrong and struggled with certain issues. After a few sessions, it was clear that she had a very busy schedule between work, dating, friends, family, and her community. Her schedule was full seven days a week, and there was little time to relax.

After a few sessions, I asked if she had ever seen the Energizer Bunny commercial where "it keeps going and going and going . . ." She chuckled, and I said, "We are not machines and we do not have a lithium battery. What do you do to replace or recharge your batteries?" She looked puzzled, sat, and thought for a few moments. She replied, "That is a good question." In that moment, she practiced self-compassion and accepted that it is okay to slow down and recharge her batteries. From that moment, Sally committed to healthier living by scheduling time for herself and allowing there to be days when she did nothing.

What have you done to recharge your own batteries recently? Physical therapist Cristy Phillips said that there are so many benefits to be gained from slowing down, which can be seen in the mind and the body. As we age, we now know that our brain continues to grow. This is what is called *neuroplasticity*. For many years, even when I was studying in graduate school, neuroscientists were not so sure about how the brain would change over time. I was first taught that neuroplasticity stops after the emerging adult stage (around ages 20 to 24). Now, we know that it does in fact continue to change as we age. Many factors impact how the brain ages, including lifestyle (diet, exercise, environment, etc.), cognitive tasks (puzzles, crosswords, reading, learning, etc.), and other psychosocial factors. Slowing down, especially within the context of mindful living, contributes to healthy aging.

As we consider the notion of healthy aging, think about retirement. This is a concept that has been lost in the West. People nowadays are working much later in life or cannot afford to retire. We do not know how to slow down and what it would be like if we did not have work. You probably know someone who became anxious when they considered retiring because they didn't know if they could afford to retire, didn't know what they would do to occupy their time, or felt so defined by their career that they couldn't imagine ending it.

When we practice slowing down proactively, rather than waiting and being reactive, we learn how to slow down on purpose rather than being forced to stop or slow down. It is hard for many of us to let go and just be. With the practice of mindfulness, you learn to be thankful for those moments, yearn for quiet time, and embrace slowing down. And with all of that commitment to slowing down, you can begin to reap the benefits of the practice of mindfulness.

De-Stress and Relax

One of the most tangible benefits of slowing down is the ability to de-stress and relax. Here are some of the many benefits of de-stressing and relaxing, from the Mayo Clinic (check out the Resources section for more on the Mayo Clinic and stress, page 161):

- Increased energy
- Decreased fatigue
- Becoming more resilient
- Less impatience
- Less irritability
- Decreased anger
- Improved physical health
- Improved mental health
- Improved memory and concentration
- Changes to brain structures
- Slowing heart rate
- Lower blood pressure
- Improved digestion
- Stable blood sugar levels
- Reduced stress hormone activity
- Reduced muscle tension and chronic pain
- Better sleep
- Improved confidence

These benefits are consistent with findings from mindfulness-based research, too, published in *Behaviour Research and Therapy*. This is often my pitch when I am working with someone who is worried or a little hesitant about starting the practice of mindfulness: there is not a person on this planet who would not wish for these benefits. The only issue is that these benefits are not totally tangible.

Things like digestion, sleep, energy, and confidence, for example, waver within an individual no matter how healthy they are. Even in their best moments, they can fluctuate. We also cannot totally and accurately measure them. Then, think about hormone activity, memory, or changes in brain structures. These are neurological constructs that scientists are still getting a better grasp of. So, while we know that these benefits are all great and no one would say no to these improvements, they are not entirely accessible to comprehend. Thus, we can't fully quantify how mindfulness can help us.

There is no doubt in my mind (or in the evidence-based research), however, that mindfulness-based practices will improve your overall well-being.

RECHARGE YOUR BATTERY

There are many benefits gained from slowing down the pace of life. On the following lines, write down all the activities that you can think of that will help you slow down and recharge your battery. (Actually, just reading and completing these exercises is one of them.) Expand on those listed in this chapter. The list can and should be comprehensive. Some examples can include taking a bath, shutting off your phone when work is done one day this week, or scheduling a massage.

BEING IN NATURE

Even if you are not someone who likes to get dirty or go for a hike, I am confident that you can find the beauty and the magic of nature. For example, have you ever watched a hummingbird feed? Or a tree sway in the wind? Or a squirrel finding an acorn? These moments allow us to slow down and enjoy life in that moment.

Find a place outside this week where you can watch nature. Just describe to yourself what you are looking at. Notice the other thoughts coming in and let them go out. Just be in nature.

INNER CHILD

Do you have any markers or crayons around? There is a growing body of evidence supporting the value of mindfulness exercises for adults such as coloring. In fact, there are studies on mindful coloring with veterans that found the practice decreased stress and anxiety and improved memory. Color the following image with whatever you have lying around. Allow thoughts to come and go, notice judgments, and simply color.

PROGRESSIVE RELAXATION

We know that mindfulness practices can help ease tension in our muscles, so let us put that to the test. In this practice, choose one part of your body where you can easily tense the muscles and then let them go. This is called progressive relaxation.

Here's one way to do it: lying down (or sitting in a chair while reading this book), focus on your right leg. Picture an energy line running from the toes to the hip. Tense your foot, then calf muscles, and then thighs. Hold it for 5 to 10 seconds. Then, slowly let the tension go, allowing your leg to fall back into the ground (or bed, or allowing your foot to fall heavier into the floor if you remain seated). Afterward, observe the calm sensations in the right leg as you let the tension go.

Just choose any area on your body, circle it on the picture, then tense the area, and release it. Keep repeating the tension and release. You can do this anywhere at any time.

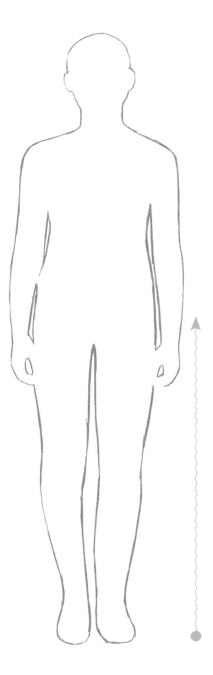

ACTIVATING YOUR SENSES

There is evidence that aromatherapy, the act of using essential oils and aromatic plant extracts, improves health and well-being. Lavender, for example, has been shown to have anti-inflammatory properties and to decrease anxiety, insomnia, and restlessness. If you can, buy a candle with lavender or, better yet, an oil diffuser. (I have found them online for less than 10 dollars these days.) Or you can find a flower or plant outside that has fragrant properties you enjoy. Just sit, lie down, or walk while smelling the object.

If you have a scented candle with relaxation properties, light that when you are able to, just watching the light and activating your smelling sense. That is mindful smelling. It allows for de-stressing and relaxation.

When practicing mindful smelling, follow these simple instructions:

◆ Sit comfortably.

◆ Remain quiet.

◆ Observe the smells.

◆ Describe the aroma.

◆ Just be. (You could also do yoga, the dishes, or other activities while paying attention to the smell.)

SLEEP HYGIENE

One important aspect of slowing down and relaxing is experiencing restful sleep (maybe the most important factor, actually). I find that I work with so many people on their sleep issues, especially in today's world. Sleep hygiene is a collection of behaviors that improve our sleep time and quality. Some basic practices of sleep hygiene include the following:

◆ Go to bed and wake up the same time each day, no matter your schedule.

◆ Create a restful and peaceful environment in your bedroom.

◆ Avoid large meals, caffeine, and high sugar foods after 7 p.m.

- Stay active during the day and exercise.
- If you do not fall asleep within 15 to 20 minutes of getting into bed, get up—no lying there counting sheep.

These techniques help condition the body so it knows that when you lie in bed, you are ready to rest and sleep.

One item missing from the list that I always add is to remove the phone from the bedroom. Use an alarm clock if needed, but do not make the excuse that you need your phone next to your bed for the alarm or in case of an emergency. The connection to the device while sleeping has created a dependency and has changed our sleep patterns.

MINDFUL MUSIC

Though listening to music so that you are not alone with your thoughts is a problem, you can also listen to music mindfully. Using your mobile device, computer, or your favorite CD/record, just listen. Ideally, you will listen to music that does not have words. As we try to separate our attachment to words, it is helpful in the practice of mindfulness to disengage from words when possible.

I search for music using keywords like mindful music, Zen meditation, spa music, relaxation, or jazz. Find some music that you enjoy, preferably with no words, and just listen. Can you commit to just listening for 10 minutes, with no devices and no distractions? You can also do this while commuting or walking in your neighborhood. Simply listen to the sounds.

WHAT DO YOU NEED?

In 1943, psychologist Abraham Maslow developed his famous Hierarchy of Needs. In this hierarchy, he claimed that humans require basic needs to be met before they can enhance their overall well-being and psychological health. This has proven to be true time and time again, and I can speak to this across all populations, institutions, and countries I have worked with. You cannot worry about love and confidence if you do not have food or a safe place to sleep. If you feel unsafe, that is not the moment to work on belonging.

Study the following diagram of the Hierarchy of Needs. On the lines to the right, see if there are some areas where you can make improvements. For example, perhaps you want to improve your sex life or increase the hours that you sleep in the first section (physiological needs) or want to open a savings account for some financial safety in the second section (safety needs). Maybe you're working on a relationship you have been avoiding for some time in the third section (love and belonging needs). Just write if there is an intention or committed action relating to each section.

Self-actualization

Esteem

Love/Belonging

Safety

Physiological

DON'T FORGET TO LAUGH

Laughing is one of the best medicines for our health, yet we often forget what it feels like to experience joy. I will share with you some things that help me laugh:

1. A favorite sketch from *Saturday Night Live* or a late night show (with Jimmy Fallon, Stephen Colbert, Jimmy Kimmel, etc.).

2. A funny YouTube video of animals doing something silly. (I feel like one of these is going around every week.)

Find something that makes you laugh. It could be a skit from a talk show, a clip from your favorite comedy film, a video of a comedian, a joke book, etc. Just laugh. Laughter boosts the immune system and creates oxytocin, the happy hormone, in the body. The more we laugh, the better we feel. What makes you laugh?

_____

_____

_____

_____

_____

_____

_____

_____

_____

_____

_____

What recent event made you laugh?

_____

_____

_____

_____

_____

SCREEN TIME

In chapter 3, we recorded our time with social media. Now, let us look at how much time we spend in front of any screen. This includes televisions, computers, mobile devices, and anything else that connects to the Internet. Write the amount of time that you are currently spending in front of those screens and then what your goal is for this coming week.

TECHNOLOGY	AMOUNT OF TIME I CURRENTLY SPEND	AMOUNT OF TIME I WANT TO SPEND NEXT WEEK
PHONE		
TV		
COMPUTER		
OTHER _____		

TAKING TIME OFF

As you finish the exercises in this chapter, are you willing to schedule time to do nothing? It is best if our days look different each week so that a day off is actually a day off and not a day when we check some emails, reply to our manager only twice, or do just one hour of work. That is not taking time off. The goal in this chapter is to realize when and where you can create space to relax and unwind. This is one of the most critical practices within mindful living. Write what you are willing to do to relax this week:

_____

_____

_____

_____

_____

_____

_____

_____

_____

_____

_____

_____

_____

_____

Chapter 8

PRACTICE GRATITUDE

Can you remember a time when you worked really hard on a project and waited for some recognition from your supervisor? It probably felt so good when it finally came—and if it never came, it probably felt pretty bad. Acknowledgment of our work or actions is validating, and many of us seek that from people in our lives. In this chapter, we will learn how the expression of gratitude is beneficial for us as well as for those we share it with. We'll also look at the positive effects gratitude has on the body and mind.

THE POWER OF A GRATITUDE PRACTICE

When I was a teenager, I was a lifeguard, which, according to *Baywatch*, is a glamorous and sexy job. In reality, some parts are glamorous, like sitting in a tall chair and yelling at kids not to run. But most of it is not. You have to clean bathrooms, pick up garbage, and remove litter from parking areas. No one talks about those things, and lifeguards get little credit for them. One day, my manager acknowledged how well I had cleaned the bathroom and thanked me. I felt appreciated. It felt especially good because there were many times when I did not receive any appreciation. That was gratitude.

Within mindfulness, gratitude requires a heightened level of awareness and intention. (Remember our discussion of intentions in chapter 4, page 48). According to Robert Emmons, gratitude is an action, an emotion, a mood, a spiritual practice, a habit or a coping skill, an intention, a trait-based characteristic of someone, and even a way of life. The action of gratitude is showing gratitude to others and to ourselves.

When it comes to gratitude, much of the focus is on how we express it to others. In the practice of mindfulness, we also consider how we practice gratitude for ourselves. (Think back to page 83, where we learned about self-compassion.) There are so many ways to express gratitude within the practice of mindfulness, such as giving compliments to others, listening with intention to a story that a loved one shares, meditating and thinking about someone who is suffering, spending time with someone in need, buying coffee for the person in line behind you, and so on. I find that the practice of gratitude allows for creativity and individuality. Acts of gratitude are like snowflakes—no two are alike. This is the case as we consider the practice of gratitude within mindfulness.

There is an emerging body of literature showing that the more we express gratitude, the more benefits we can reap. These benefits include reduction in stress, higher levels of happiness, healthier relationships, improved sleep, and better performance in life, school, or career. In one 2018 study, participants who reported higher levels of gratitude as well as mindfulness presented significantly fewer symptoms of depression and anxiety. There is also evidence that as we practice gratitude, we are able to release negative and unhealthy emotions. We do not have to share gratitude or say it aloud to reap these benefits, which occur over time.

These practices have a tremendous impact on our sense of self and overall peace and can even change parts of our brain structures. A 2016 study showed that the medial prefrontal cortex region, the part of the brain involved in learning and decision-making, shows activity when we express gratitude or remember a time we expressed it. Those researchers concluded that this is because people who express gratitude are more aware of their behaviors, which likely accounts for many of the improved health outcomes.

Another important part of gratitude is the sense of self. Many people come to mindfulness after years of self-criticism. Inside, we have many negative experiences swirling around like a tornado. Gratitude creates space to respect and then release this tornado of thought and emotion. The acceptance and release of this negativity improves many aspects of well-being. This even includes improvements to our cardiovascular health. In fact, Stephen Gallagher and colleagues found that it was the specific moment of gratitude, not the personality trait of frequently engaging with gratitude, that lowered blood pressure. That suggests that, more than having a positive and thankful personality, being able to demonstrate and focus on gratitude in moments of stress can be very beneficial.

These practices take time to become integrated into our biological functioning. It would be unreasonable to expect to show gratitude today and then feel amazing tomorrow. It is important to begin by becoming aware of opportunities to express thanks to someone and to embrace your own accomplishments.

Mindful Gratitude

By now, you understand that within the practice of mindfulness, everything we do is done with awareness, attention, and purpose. This is also true for gratitude. Practicing gratitude doesn't mean becoming a doormat and letting others take advantage of you. Instead, it means practicing moments of thanks and appreciation for both the positive and the negative moments in your life. The practices in this chapter will provide opportunities to cultivate gratitude in your life, both internally and externally. Remember, these practices can take time and we are training our brains to become stronger. Approach one practice at a time.

Before we start practicing, consider whether any of these benefits of gratitude are things you could benefit from:

◆ Improved physical and psychological health

◆ Improved sleep

◆ Increased empathy

◆ Reduced irritation and aggression

◆ Improved social connection and healthier relationships

◆ Enhanced self-esteem

◆ Better performance in school or career

◆ Reduced stress

◆ Higher levels of happiness

DEFINING GRATITUDE

Have you had a teacher or coach who was instrumental in your life? Without knowing it, you have likely practiced gratitude toward that person. Gratitude can be expressed in the form of a behavior (overt) or performed unconsciously or mindfully (covert). It is possible that we can express gratitude for someone without even knowing it, in a dream, or through a memory (e.g., seeing your child's teacher or coach may remind you of one of your own from childhood). In this practice, we want to make gratitude more overt and conscious. So, we will start by defining it. On the following lines, write the first 10 words that come to mind as you consider what gratitude means to you.

_____

_____

_____

_____

_____

_____

_____

_____

_____

_____

Now, think of two people with whom you have had positive experiences. Write a sentence thanking them. Be sure to acknowledge what they did for you or what you have learned from them.

_____

_____

_____

_____

_____

_____

_____

_____

_____

THREE GOOD THINGS

Gratitude doesn't erase the negative moments, but it does help shift focus onto the positive. We often focus on negative things and forget to celebrate positive moments because our brains are hardwired to recall negative moments more vividly. In the following area, write about three things that happened in the past year that were good. This could include completing a task at work, finishing a large project for school, enrolling a child in camp, giving a speech, winning a game (or making one good play during a game you lost), pulling the weeds in the front yard, adopting a pet, having a child, being held by a parent before they passed, or anything else. Just write three good things.

1. _____

2. _____

3. _____

THANK-YOU NOTES

Do you remember a time when people wrote cards and sent them in the mail? My best friend still sends birthday and thank-you cards. When I receive those cards, it feels good. It also makes her feel good to send them.

Write a list of people you could send a card to in the coming weeks:

◆ _____

◆ _____

◆ _____

◆ _____

◆ _____

Then, consider whether you will actually write and send the cards. Remember, the act of expressing gratitude, even internally, creates the same benefits. Think of the pros and cons of sending the cards and then, in this moment, you can decide whether to send.

PROS FOR SENDING	CONS FOR SENDING	SEND? (YES OR NO)
Maria is lonely and it might make her feel good to receive mail.	Stamps costs 55 cents.	Yes!

HAPPINESS JAR

Find a jar or something in your house that can hold small pieces of paper (e.g., a shoe box, a memory box). Set a period of time, such as from the coming week, to the coming month, or even this whole year, and commit to writing down moments when you felt gratitude during this time. Write these moments as regularly as possible when you notice them. Place the pieces of paper in the jar. Then, at least one or two times per year, open the jar and read the pieces of paper.

GRATEFUL FOR CHALLENGES

Mindfulness doesn't erase challenges, but it can help you build relationships with the challenges and create space to honor them. By acknowledging them, we manage the emotions related to the challenges, rather than letting the challenges manage us. In the following section, write at least one challenge you have faced during the past year. Feel free to write as many challenges as you wish. Then, create a message of thanks for that challenge.

CHALLENGES	THANK YOU, CHALLENGES
DIVORCE	If it were not for the divorce, which was very painful to experience, I would not have learned how to love myself unconditionally. I can now reflect on the nights that I cried and realize that I was able to see the unhealthiness in the marriage. I also learned that I am able to love, and I feel that I will love more fully in my next romantic relationship.

CONSIDER VOLUNTEERING

Part I: To Volunteer or Not: That Is the Question

Volunteering has been shown to improve our well-being and have positive effects on our sense of self. Whether you're working at a food pantry, mentoring some students, or weeding a community garden, volunteering helps you connect with others, see the world from other perspectives, and take values-driven actions.

On the following lines, list some agencies or places where you can volunteer in your neighborhood. It could be a homeless shelter, a food pantry, an animal shelter, a child advocacy program, etc. Find something that aligns with your values. For example, if you value animal welfare, volunteer at an animal shelter. If you value the environment, sign up to compost. If you value social justice, offer to make calls or send texts to get out the vote.

1. _____

2. _____

3. _____

4. _____

5. _____

Part II: Benefits of Volunteering

Why do 25% of adults volunteer? What are the benefits of volunteering? And if you haven't volunteered, why haven't you? There are obstacles to all beneficial actions in life, so let us identify both the reasons you might want to volunteer and the reasons you might have to not volunteer. As you write them both down, you may see that the cons are not as big or powerful as they seemed in your mind, especially compared to the pros.

PROS FOR VOLUNTEERING	CONS
Help a cause I care about	Driving to the shelter after work will take 25 minutes

GRATITUDE LETTERS

Writing a gratitude letter can help release negative emotion, increase activity in the medial prefrontal cortex of the brain, and much more.

To write a gratitude letter, start by thinking of someone for whom you are thankful and to whom you have not expressed your gratitude. It can even be yourself. Address the letter to that person and do the following:

- Just write about how they impacted you.

- Do not focus on grammar or style.

- Be specific about what the person did for you.

- Describe the emotions you felt when that person did what they did, and even describe the emotions you feel today as you write this letter.

- Consider how this person has impacted who you are today.

Just like in the Thank-You Notes exercise (page 118), you can decide whether you actually deliver this letter. You could mail it, give it to them in person, read it aloud over the phone or video, or just hold it in your room. It is yours to share or keep private.

MINDFUL MEDITATION FOR GRATITUDE

How is your meditation practice going? Here's a gratitude meditation that you can try. This script asks you to focus on someone who has had an impact on your life.

1. Find a comfortable seat and sit with your spine super straight, crown of the head to the ceiling, feet grounded firmly on the earth (or buttocks on the cushion).

2. Take three deep breaths. As you inhale, push your belly out like a balloon. When you exhale, bring your belly button back to the spine.

3. Bringing the attention onto your heart area and think of someone who has had a tremendous impact on your life. It could be a romantic partner, sibling, parent, grandparent, mentor, teacher, or anyone else.

4. With your attention in your heart area, see if you can create an image of that person. Can you see their face?

5. Smile and say, "Thank you," or any phrase that feels like it fits in this practice. Repeat this as many times as you like.

6. Take a few more breaths as you keep this person and this image close to your heart. Keep the smile on your face. Try to hold it for three minutes or longer.

7. Open your eyes and see what you notice.

REFLECTING ON GRATITUDE

In the Mindful Meditation for Gratitude exercise (page 125), you thought about someone to whom you wanted to express gratitude. Now, write how you felt after you
opened your eyes. Remember, do not judge your emotions or thoughts. Just write
what you felt. It is okay if you felt better, felt nothing, or even felt worse. Just notice
and describe how you feel.

_____

_____

_____

_____

_____

_____

_____

_____

_____

_____

_____

_____

_____

_____

_____

THE GRATITUDE GAME

As you share gratitude with yourself and others, consider playing this game, an adaptation of the game Pictionary. In this version, players draw something that they are thankful for. The same rules apply: no words, letters, or numbers, and you have 60 seconds to guess the other person's drawing. You can also incorporate any other rules (e.g., no acting out, no speaking). Give it a try at your next dinner party or family event.

Practice here: Draw two objects that represent things that you are thankful for.

Chapter 9

CREATE SPACE FOR JOY

As we grow in our understanding and practice of mindfulness, we become increasingly aware of how we feel in the present moment, notice our thoughts and emotions more accurately, and begin to create space for joy. Many of us come to the practice of mindfulness because of suffering, which means we are looking for happiness. What have you done to create happiness and joy in your life? In this chapter, we will learn more about these emotions and explore ways to make more room for experiences of joy.

MAKE SPACE FOR JOY AND HAPPINESS

When is the last time you felt joy? This is a question that I ask many clients. Usually, people sift through their memories and come up with an event a few months or even years ago. Or even worse, they respond, "I don't know. I can't think of anything." Take a few minutes and ask yourself, when did you last feel joy?

Joy is a constant and internal feeling, one of contentment and peace. Joy is a celebration of your successes, well-being, and good fortune. It can be a lot of work to create joy. Joy often requires change. Creating joy means committing to taking action toward healthier living: staying active, sleeping regularly, focusing on thoughts, and accepting negativity, for starters. Change is hard, but isn't it worth it?

Feelings of joy have many positive effects on the mind and body, including boosting our immune systems, overcoming and coping effectively with stress, reducing our blood pressure, and even extending our lives. There is also a ton of research that has shown that being happy can reduce the pain we experience in our daily lives, a point that has also been observed in studies about Mindfulness-Based Stress Reduction (MBSR).

Before we look at using mindfulness to increase joy, it is helpful to differentiate some of the terms we use to describe moments of joy, such as happiness and contentment. Joy is more of a trait, a part of your personality, created internally as you find peace in your life. Happiness is the external expression of joy and includes the celebration of well-being and contentment, like laughing with a group of good friends. Contentment connotes a feeling of satisfaction. Many clients are turned off by this word; some may feel that to be content means to accept mediocrity or being average. But this is not true. Contentment is being happy with what you have in the moment, not deciding that you never want anything else. And, frankly, average is really good. Fifty percent of the population is average, and that is a healthy place to be. However, many of us yearn for more while not enjoying what we have in the present moment, and those desires create internal angst. When you can create a place of acceptance and describe contentment, you have joy. No matter the term, the evidence is clear that all of these feelings produce positive impacts on our overall well-being.

Evidence shows that mindfulness helps create and increase joy. One group of researchers found that the practices of meditation and self-compassion increased happiness and could actually predict how happy people would feel. And, as subjects meditated more, their levels of happiness increased.

Keeping in mind the definitions we discussed, mindfulness is one of the best tools to create that internal peace and constant feeling of joy. It opens opportunities to feel happy and nonjudgmentally allows us to be content with where we are in this moment with conscious intentions. Mindfulness brings focus by increasing our awareness and creates space for joy.

Celebrate Positives

As we discussed on page 118, being able to celebrate the positives is a huge component of creating joy, and mindfulness amplifies positives. This means that mindfulness allows us to celebrate all of the tiny victories.

I was speaking with a client who was distressed following an altercation with a family member. He was worried that the family member was engaging in unhealthy and risky behaviors. He expressed care and concern to the family member, but he was invalidated and ignored. Notably, this altercation occurred right at the end of a lovely week-long family vacation. The client could not see any of the positives from the week; instead, he focused on this one problem.

Mindfulness does not erase negative moments. However, it does allow for us to give energy to the positive moments in an intentional manner. It's kind of like overriding the brain. In this example, the brain was pulling the client to focus on the fight because it was a situation filled with intense emotion and he felt helpless. The practice of mindfulness reminds him that he also had a week of vacation, that this moment will pass, and that observing his worry and frustration is more effective than engaging in this emotional tornado.

The following exercises will begin the process of creating joy in your life, build this relationship between the practice of mindfulness and happiness, and create space for you to celebrate positives.

CELEBRATE POSITIVES

In the following section, write down one positive from the past month. Then, think about one from the past year. Finally, think of one of the best moments in your life up until this point.

Moment from the past month:

_____

_____

Moment from the past year:

_____

_____

Best positive moment to date:

_____

_____

This practice is an attempt to raise awareness to the positive experiences. We all always have something positive that we can write, but finding it might require that you let go of the negative that may be interfering with your joy. In the past month, you probably woke up and completed at least one chore. That could be a positive. Maybe you talked to a friend you had not spoken to in quite some time. That could also be a positive. Release the negative and find these positive moments; there are always silver linings.

PEOPLE WHO BRING ME JOY

All of us have those people in our lives: the ones who make us smile when they enter the room. In this exercise, think about who in your life brings you joy. Animals count, too! Just write the names of those people or animals in your life that make you smile.

The simple act of writing their names will help remind you of the feelings of joy they evoke.

1. _____

2. _____

3. _____

4. _____

5. _____

MAKING TIME TO BE HAPPY

As you work to release negativity and make space to celebrate positivity, can you commit to engaging with at least one or two of the people or animals that you listed in the previous exercise? This is the part of joy that requires work. You might notice that you make excuses, feel anxiety or fear, and just want to remain in your current state. In the following two-week schedule, write down one activity, phone call, or other type of communication that you will commit to with at least one (but preferably two) of the people from your list.

	MINDFULNESS PRACTICE TIME
MONDAY	
TUESDAY	
WEDNESDAY	
THURSDAY	
FRIDAY	
SATURDAY	
SUNDAY	

	MINDFULNESS PRACTICE TIME
MONDAY	
TUESDAY	
WEDNESDAY	
THURSDAY	
FRIDAY	
SATURDAY	
SUNDAY	

MOVIE NIGHT

As you build this relationship with yourself and your emotions, take a moment to celebrate the work you've accomplished. I recommend celebrating by watching the Disney Pixar movie *Inside Out*. The movie focuses on the basic emotions and depicts them as characters that we all can connect with. It helps educate children; however, it is made for adults, too. (Several mental health professionals acted as consultants on the film.) As you watch the film, you can sit back and observe your emotions, just as you do in mindfulness. See if you can connect with the character called Joy, and consider whether there is someone you wish to watch this movie with.

Alternatively, if you have another movie that makes you laugh, go ahead and watch that. The goal is to create space for happiness, to smile, and to just be. Following the movie, write down some reflections about the role of joy and mindfulness in your life.

_____

_____

_____

_____

_____

_____

HEALTHY HABIT REVIEW

Let's look at which of your joy-fostering behaviors have become habits. The following sections provide some examples of healthy and positive habits that might create more joy in your life. See if you can write your own list. If you cannot, use this exercise to make at least one commitment to one healthy and positive habit you can start today.

Daily:
Example: walking, one healthy meal, journaling, meditating, prayer, exercise

_____

_____

_____

Monthly:
Example: a retreat, yoga, exercise, attending a religious ceremony, a family dinner, socializing with friends

_____

_____

_____

Yearly:
Example: a vacation, time off from work, a family reunion, a comic book convention

_____

_____

_____

SMILE ON PURPOSE

Sometimes, this exercise feels awkward, even for me. But smiling on purpose—smiling because you have made the decision to smile rather than in reaction to something in your environment—works. So when I think of the cost-benefit ratio, I decide it makes the most sense to smile on purpose. I would rather enjoy the benefits of inner peace, happiness, and joy over the cost of looking silly and feeling awkward.

The next time you are on the phone with a customer service representative and feeling frustrated, smile. When you are cut off while driving, smile. When you are late and on a crowded train or bus, smile. You get it.

Write down what you notice as you practice this. You can even try smiling while reading this.

THE POWER OF COMPLIMENTS

Write down five compliments you could give to people in your life.

Example: *To my partner, you were supportive yesterday when I shared that I was scared to go on vacation next week. Thank you for being there and supporting me.*

_____

_____

_____

_____

_____

_____

_____

_____

_____

_____

_____

_____

_____

_____

_____

_____

_____

_____

The more compliments we give, the more space we create for joy. We create the space to share small victories with people in our lives, which allows for both of us to benefit.

DECLUTTER YOUR LIFE

Organizing your life—decluttering, both mentally and physically—can make more space for joy. There is evidence that our external environment matches our internal processes, so if we can declutter items in our environment, we simplify our internal thoughts and emotions. But we often put off decluttering because it doesn't seem as pressing as all our other to-dos. This exercise aims to help you get organized and declutter spaces so that you have more time to focus on what brings you joy.

In the following section, write down your to-do list on the left-hand side. You can write it for today or for the week. On the right side, write down decluttering projects that you have been wanting to complete (e.g., sorting through some old magazines you no longer look at, DVDs you do not watch, etc.). For each to-do item you complete, make sure to complete one item from the declutter list, as well. You may notice that decluttering did not take as much time as you thought and brought as much value into your life as many of the things on the to-do list.

TO-DO LIST	DECLUTTER LIST

YOUR STORY

There is research in CBT that writing and editing our stories can create joy. We all have a story of who we are. Many aspects of that story include attachments to people and identities. For example, my story includes being a professor, a student of Buddhism, a psychologist, and an athlete. As I reflect on being a professor, my story includes 12 years of graduate school and a terminal PhD degree. That is a thing, an attachment.

Take a moment to reflect on your story. Who are you, what are you attached to, and what is your story?

Now, in the following section, rewrite your story as if it were being told by the observer within (the one that we are cultivating through these mindfulness practices). Think about how you would tell the story of a friend. Based on my previous example about my graduate studies and professor identity, I would write: *Earning a PhD is a lot of work, and most people feel stress and resentment about positive and overly com-mitted actions. Today, you help and train so many people. Your degree has provided you the opportunity to help people during their journey of healing.* Now, you try.

THE RESILIENCE LINING

In the Celebrate Positives exercise (page 132), I asked you to think about silver linings. As we experience negative emotions and practice letting them go, we realize that we are able to learn something with every experience, no matter how difficult or even traumatic. Let's try thinking of this as the *resilience lining*.

Reflect on some challenging experiences and find the learning moment from them. Being able to learn from negativity promotes growth and will create resilience. Let's create your resilience lining.

EVENT	LEARNED
Car accident	I should always pull over when tired and be aware at intersection X. I have skills to organize paperwork and deal with the insurance companies.

Chapter 10

EMBRACE YOUR EMOTIONS

No matter how mindful you become, emotions are powerful experiences that can sometimes take over. This is especially true during times of vulnerability or high stress. In these times, we regress to a biological state that is focused on protection and we lose the effective coping skills that we have learned and practiced. This final chapter will dive deeper into the role of emotions as they relate to mindfulness and reinforce strategies for how to manage our emotions and eliminate any attempt of trying to control how we feel.

ENGAGE WITH YOUR EMOTIONS

Many clients come to therapy after years of avoiding their emotions. There are many strategies that people use to avoid their emotions. Some are healthy, like long-distance running, and others are less healthy, like drinking alcohol. But when we practice mindfulness, we embrace what is, including our emotions. We accept emotions and thoughts as fleeting moments in time. Our emotions are like waves in the ocean that come in and go out. The practice of mindfulness trains our brain to watch feelings come in and go out without attaching to them.

We are not what we feel. Feelings are not dangerous. Feelings are evolutionary and protective, and we strengthen our ability to engage with all of our emotions through mindfulness. No matter how positive, negative, strong, or weak they are, we simply engage with our emotions.

As we learn to let our thoughts float on clouds, drift down the river, or just go around the racetrack, we understand that we are not what we feel. In Buddhism, this is the notion of impermanence as well as the universality of suffering. Nothing is forever. No one wants to feel sadness or anger, yet we all do to some degree at various points in our lives. The key is that when you feel them, you observe them as emotions but do not identify with them.

Do you know a person who is always negative? This might be a coworker, a family member, or a neighbor. Each time you see them, they are quick to tell you all their health problems, list who is sick or has died, or weigh in on all the problems in the world. Over time, they may have overidentified with their negative emotions. Of course, depression is a medical diagnosis and, as we saw in chapter 1, is one of the most common mental health disorders in the world. However, just because I feel sadness does not mean that I am depressed. Rather, within the practice of mindfulness, we accept that sadness, along with all other emotions, is a fleeting, impermanent experience and that you are not what you feel. Our emotions are perfect just the way they are. They are more perfect when we engage with them in a healthy manner, but we do not hold on to them.

Finally, as we describe and engage with our emotions, we are strengthening our ability to feel emotions effectively. Many of us have likely come to this book because we are trying to create happiness and release negative emotions. Within mindfulness, we experience emotions fully as though they are unique colors, textures, tastes, smells, and sounds. We involve all of our senses as we give them space to grow. We are no longer afraid of them. Some of us fear positivity because it means negativity will follow. Some work hard to avoid emotions altogether. Remember, we are not what we feel, emotions have very important purposes, and the practice of mindfulness strengthens our ability to embrace them.

Release the Need to Control Your Thoughts and Emotions

There is no mechanism in this life that allows us to control how we feel. The closest thing might be some medications or mind-altering drugs, but even with them, we still feel emotions. Mindfulness trains our brain to manage and recognize our emotions rather than attempt to control.

Imagine that you are on the 51st floor of a New York City skyscraper and there is a small balcony. Even if you are a thrill-seeker, there is a piece of you that feels a tinge of anxiety or excitement, a rush in your stomach or chest, as you walk onto that balcony. What if you tried to control that emotion? You would push it away, pour another glass of wine, or try to use thoughts like "I am not scared" or "I will not fall." As we release the need to control our emotions, we describe that we feel excited or nervous, give some descriptive words to the feeling (sweaty palms, adrenaline, dizziness), walk out, and accept what we feel. That is releasing control of emotion.

When I work with clients around their emotional intelligence, one of the first things we work on is eliminating the word "control" from their vocabulary. Even the most talented and mindful person cannot control their emotions. To fully benefit from the practice of mindfulness, the goal needs to be to release control of your emotions and thoughts. Emotions, just like thoughts, will come and go. Begin to think of them as a houseguest that you enjoy for the first few nights, but by the end of their stay, you are ready to let them go. You cannot control them; rather, you invite them into your home, entertain them for a set period of time, and then you wave goodbye as they leave.

Letting go of control helps foster inner peace and develops new skills that will help you interact with the people around you. This book has been your first step to freeing yourself from any internal experiences that have been holding you back and to becoming more in touch with yourself. Just as we have done in each chapter, now is the time to practice, this time building healthy emotions and emotional boundaries.

SEE YOURSELF THROUGH SOMEONE ELSE'S EYES

While we don't focus on how we are judged, it can be helpful to gather some data from those around us. Who do you trust most in life? Write down that person's name.

_____

Now, could you ask that person how they see you? If you cannot, or if you're not comfortable doing it, place yourself in their shoes and consider what they would say. How would they describe you in general, and especially as it relates to your emotions?

_____

_____

_____

_____

How do you wish to be described? Write down how you want this person to see you.

_____

_____

_____

_____

Perspective-taking, or seeing ourselves through someone else's eyes, helps us accept who we are in this moment and provides an opportunity to commit to change. As you think of your own emotional identity, what are some things that you want to change? Hopefully, you capture that person in the last part of this exercise.

EMOTIONAL INTELLIGENCE QUIZ

I label my emotions accurately and as they are.	True	False
I am aware of my strengths and weaknesses.	True	False
I easily calm myself down.	True	False
I have been told that I am a good listener.	True	False
I am able to move on when I get very frustrated.	True	False
I know how to build rapport with others.	True	False
I regularly ask others for feedback on how I can improve.	True	False

If you answered "true" to two or more of these items, you have some emotional intelligence. However, we can all benefit from more and continued growth. To take a more comprehensive quiz, see the Resources page for a complete and free quiz offered by MindTools (page 161).

LETTING GO

Sometimes people hurt us. All of us have learned how to let it go. While time is often one of the best factors for truly letting things go, perhaps we can learn some other behaviors that help. For example, sometimes I go to the gym, take a long walk, eat some Oreos, or speak with a friend.

Each of the following questions asks you to think of a negative or challenging experience and consider how to let it go.

Think of a time when you were in a group and you took a stand or had an opinion that was not shared by others. How did you feel?

What did it take to let go of the fact that they did not share your view?

_____

_____

_____

Think of a time when someone hurt your feelings. How did you feel?

_____

_____

_____

What did it take to let go of your hurt feelings?

_____

_____

_____

Can you recall a time when a family member or partner said something hurtful? What did that feel like?

_____

_____

_____

_____

How did you let those feelings go?

_____

_____

_____

Think of a time when a coworker criticized your work. How did it feel?

_____

_____

_____

How did you handle that?

_____

_____

_____

Reflect on your answers. Did you notice a theme on practices you use to let go of emotion?

_____

_____

_____

_____

MINDFUL EMOTIONS

Keeping the experiences and emotions from the Letting Go exercise in mind, let's practice mindful emotions. This is a meditative practice that will allow you to create space for those emotions and raise awareness.

1. As with all mindful practices, get in a comfortable and strong seated position. Close your eyes if you feel comfortable doing so, or lower your gaze onto the floor.

2. Allow for three deep breaths where you push your belly button out like your belly is a balloon being inflated. Then, allow for your belly button to come back to your spine.

3. Consider some of the experiences and emotions that you wrote about in Letting Go. Can you create those feelings? Describe them.

4. As you inhale, give space for those emotions. When you exhale, picture them leaving your body. Really focus on the inhale, extending your belly button out like a balloon being inflated.

5. Allow three to five minutes for these feelings and breathings.

6. Once you have reached the end of the time, take three more of those deep belly breaths. We often begin and end with the same grounding breaths.

Write judgments about this exercise here:

_____

_____

_____

_____

_____

_____

RAIN

There are many acronyms in the world of mindfulness and psychology, and one that was developed by many Buddhist teachers years ago is RAIN.

R: recognize what is happening

A: allow life to be just as it is

I: investigate inner experiences with kindness

N: nonidentification

It has since been adapted by Tara Brach, a published Buddhist scholar and mindfulness practitioner.

Choose a recent event that caused you to experience intense emotion. It does not always have to be negative. For example, maybe you recently felt joy over meeting a new romantic interest. Those feelings of joy can lead to obsessional thinking, dependency, and overkill of emotion. The practice of RAIN helps us unlearn responding to our emotions and allows us to slow down and discover new ways to manage emotion.

R: What do you recognize is happening with this experience with intense emotion?

_____

_____

_____

_____

A: Allowing feelings to be is like learning radical acceptance (page 72). Write about how you practice allowing life to just be. How do you allow space for your emotions and experiences?

_____

_____

_____

_____

_____

_____

_____

I: Investigating is the curiosity with which you approach all of these mindful practices. What is drawing the most attention right now? How are you feeling it in your body (i.e., physical sensations)?

_____

_____

_____

_____

_____

N: Nonidentification is critical in mindfulness and in life. We are not our emotions. What is the result you are seeking from this book and in your curiosity about mindfulness?

_____

_____

_____

_____

_____

Consider this acronym the next time you experience emotions that are uncomfortable or intense. The goal is to create effective relationships with your inner self. These kinds of practices help.

EXPRESS YOURSELF

In the book *Changing Emotions*, there are many references to the impact that mindfulness can have on emotional expression and overall emotional awareness. One exercise that is often used is expressive writing. So far, we have written letters and scenarios. Now, let's try creative writing.

Think about the movie producer in your mind. How creative is this producer? In the following section, please write a short story using expressive and creative language. Focus on the emotions of the character(s). I will provide a short example.

Maurice had been excited and optimistic to begin his senior year. He had dedicated his entire high school and college career to basketball and sacrificed social and family events. He even described missing his brother's wedding in Aruba since it occurred during championship season. He was sad but had joy for his brother from afar. Then, he suffered a tragic loss of his best friend after a battle with cancer. Maurice recognized feelings of grief and knew that his friend, Roberto, wanted him to chase his dreams. That year, Maurice dedicated each game and shot to Roberto, and he was ecstatic to be named conference player of the year.

_____

_____

_____

_____

Now, grab a highlighter or pen and mark each emotion. What do you notice?

Continue to observe and develop your emotional vocabulary. The more creative and aware we are about our emotions, the more mindful of our emotional experience we become.

REFLECTIVE VALUES LISTENING

Some values ask a lot of you and others do not. For example, education can require a time commitment and money to pay college tuition, but leisure can involve something as small as a barbecue. Here are some of the values we have assessed throughout this book.

- Community
- Education
- Family
- Friends and socializing
- Parenting
- Recreation and physical activity
- Romantic relationships
- Self-care
- Spirituality or religion
- Work

No matter how big or small the value is, take this time to reflect on one and the emotions it creates for you.

Choose one of these values and write it here:

_____

_____

What feelings do you notice when you reflect on this value?

_____

_____

EMOTIONAL INTENSITY

All the way back in chapter 1, we talked about the six basic emotions: anger, disgust, fear, joy, sadness, and surprise. We are constantly experiencing emotions. Sometimes those feelings are stronger than others, and sometimes we manage them better than other times. Daniel Goleman stated that everything you've done up to this point has made you more aware of those emotions in your life and improved your Emotional Intelligence.

This exercise acknowledges when you felt these emotions and how you manage them and provides insight into behaviors that might help as you experience them again in the future.

In the following chart, describe events during the past month when you felt these basic emotions, and rate them on a scale from 1 to 10 in terms of intensity (1 being not too bad, and 10 being super intense).

EMOTION	EVENT	INTENSITY RATING 1 TO 10
ANGER		
DISGUST		
FEAR		
JOY		
SADNESS		
SURPRISE		

As you work toward greater emotional awareness and gain control of your behavior and responses, think about what you could have done differently to manage the emotions that you described. Let's think about each emotion again.

EMOTION	HOW YOU'LL HANDLE IT NEXT TIME
ANGER	
DISGUST	
FEAR	
JOY	
SADNESS	
SURPRISE	

WEATHERING THE STORM

When it comes to emotions, we all weather storms. Some come with high winds, thunder, lightning, and torrential rain. Others pass by. The clients I work with most often experience anxiety or depression. In fact, there is a lot of evidence that these two emotions go hand in hand. With mindfulness, you have the chance to watch the clouds and rain pass by. You have the ability to monitor the storm's intensity. That's why mindfulness is one of the best tools to manage anxiety and depression.

In the following space, draw a storm. Get creative. Use color if you have it. Take your time and just draw and color a storm.

Reflection: How did you feel as you drew this storm?

_____

_____

_____

_____

_____

_____

SCHEDULE: YOU MADE IT!

As we come to the end of this book, consider how you will schedule future mindfulness practices. The hope is that the practice of mindfulness becomes integrated into your being, just as deeply as breathing. Like any good routine, we have to continue to practice for it to become habit or second nature. Consider how often you can practice mindfulness, with the intentional goal of practicing daily for at least 10 to 15 minutes. If you can get to 30 minutes a few times per week, that is also wonderful.

Monday   Tuesday   Wednesday   Thursday   Friday   Saturday   Sunday

CONCLUSION: STAY CURIOUS

Each time we practice mindfulness, it is as though we are doing so for the first time. That is the beginner's mind: viewing things as if for the first time, like an alien on a new planet. As you grow through mindfulness, remember that we all have an inner child. Children are so curious about new things, and each time they engage in an activity, it is as though they are doing so for the first time. Just like that child, you must stay curious. You do not have to be perfect. Release judgments of your experiences, stay committed, ride the waves, embrace all that is, and remember to smile.

Finishing this book is a victory. Remember to stay in the present moment and celebrate all of your accomplishments, no matter how big or small. You will have times when the practice slips. When that happens, create new intentions as though it is the first time you're coming to mindfulness. There will be other moments when you get tied up in your thoughts and feelings. Like riding a bike, you come back to the practice. We smile and feel humility as we are reminded of our vulnerability.

Each day, you can remember to smile and say, "Joy," as you picture it in your heart, as you celebrate the calm feelings and kindness. Mindfulness integrates all of your senses so that you fully experience life. Remember, "full" does not mean "busy." I hope that you create space to relax. You do not have to be scheduled and busy all the time. By this point, I hope that you have created space for a daily mindfulness practice: just a small moment (or 15 minutes) to be thankful, to practice, and to embrace your emotions. This practice is lifelong and is a marathon, not a sprint.

We've got this. This is a statement I find myself repeating over and over with clients, family members, and loved ones across the globe. It might not be easy and it definitely will not be perfect, but as long as we stay curious, we've got this!

RESOURCES

The Association for Contextual and Behavioral Sciences' (ACBS) guide to Acceptance and Commitment Therapy (ACT): contextualscience.org/act_for_the_public

Brené Brown's definitions for BRAVING: DareToLead.BreneBrown.com /wp-content/uploads/2018/10/BRAVING.pdf

Calm, an app for meditation: Calm.com

The Counseling and Wellness Center, LLC: thecwcnj.com/counseling
Cognitive distortions: thecwcnj.com/pdf/Cognitive-Distortions_CWC_Burns.pdf
Sleep hygiene: thecwcnj.com/pdf/Info-sleep-hygiene.pdf
Values: thecwcnj.com/pdf/Value-Living-Questionnaire_WIlson_CWC.pdf

Emotional Intelligence Quiz from MindTools: MindTools.com/pages/article /ei-quiz.htm

Exercises from Russ Harris's *Happiness Trap*: TheHappinessTrap.com/upimages /Complete_Worksheets_2014.pdf

Guide to cortisol from WebMD: WebMD.com/a-to-z-guides/what-is-cortisol#1

Guide to relaxation techniques from the Mayo Clinic: MayoClinic.org/healthy-lifestyle /stress-management/in-depth/relaxation-technique/art-20045368

Headspace, an app for meditation: Headspace.com

Kristin Neff's Self-Compassion Quiz: Self-Compassion.org/test-how-self -compassionate-you-are

Mindfulness-Based Stress Reduction: mbsrtraining.com/jon-kabat-zinn

Tara Brach, Buddhist scholar and mindfulness practitioner: TaraBrach.com

REFERENCES

Allport, Gordon. Preface to *Man's Search for Meaning*, by Victor Frankl, 9. Boston: Beacon Press, 1964.

Atia, Merfat, and Lobna Sallam. "The Effectiveness of Mindfulness Training Techniques on Stress, Anxiety, and Depression of Depressed Patient." *American Journal of Nursing Research*, 8, no. 1 (2020): 103–113. doi: 10.12691/Ajnr-8-1-11.

Brach, Tara. *True Refuge: Finding Peace and Freedom in Your Own Awakened Heart.* London: Bantam, 2013.

Boggiss, Anna, Nathan Consedine, Jennifer Brenton-Peters, Paul Hofman, and Anna Serlachius. "A Systematic Review of Gratitude Interventions: Effects on Physical Health and Health Behaviors." *Research* 135 (2020). doi: 10.1016/J.Jpsychores.2020.110165.

Brantley, Jeffrey. *Calming Your Anxious Mind: How Mindfulness and Compassion Can Free You from Anxiety, Fear, and Panic* (2nd Ed.). Oakland, CA: New Harbinger Publications, 2007.

Brown, Brené. *Daring Greatly.* New York: Gotham Books, 2012.

Burns, David. *The Feeling Good Handbook.* New York: William Morrow and Company, Inc, 1989.

Campos, Daniel, Ausiàs Cebolla, Soledad Quero, Juani Breton-Lopez, Christina Botella, Joaquim Soler, Javier Garcia-Campayo, Marcelo Demarzo, and Rosa M Baños. "Meditation and Happiness: Mindfulness and Self-Compassion May Mediate the Meditation-Happiness Relationship." *Personality and Individual Differences* 93 (2016): 80–85. doi: 10.1016/J.Paid.2015.08.040.

Cassiello-Robbins, Clair, Shannon Sauer-Zavala, Leslie R. Brody, and David Barlow. "Exploring the Effects of the Mindfulness and Countering Emotional Behaviors Modules from the Unified Protocol on Dysregulated Anger in the Context of Emotional Disorders." *Behavior Therapy* 51, no. 6 (2020). doi: 10.1016/J.Beth.2019.12.007.

Chödrön, Pema. *Awakening Loving-Kindness.* Boston, MA: Shambhala Publishing, 1996.

Chödrön, Pema. *The Places That Scare You*. Boston, MA: Shambhala Publishing, 2001.

Chopra, Deepak. Author. Total Meditation: Practices in Living the Awakened Life. Potter/Ten Speed/Harmony/Rodale, 2020.

Cohen, Sheldon, William J. Doyle, Ronald B. Turner, Cuneyt M. Alper, and David P. Skoner. "Emotional Style and Susceptibility to the Common Cold." *Psychosom Med* 65, no. 4 (2003): 652–657. doi: 10.1097/01.Psy.0000077508.57784.Da.

Dalai Lama, His Holiness the 14th. *Beyond Religion: Ethics for the Whole World*. Boston, MA: Mariner Books, 2012.

Dogen, Zenji. *Shobogenzo Chapter 11—Uji: Time-Present: A Modern Interpretation*. Translated by M. Eido Luetchford. 2004. DogenSangha.org.uk/Talks/11-Uji%20 Interpretation.pdf.

Dumoulin, Heinrich. *Zen Buddhism: A History. Volume 2: Japan*. Bloomington, IN: World Wisdom, Inc., 2005.

Duprey, Erinn B., Laura McKee, C. W. O'Neal, and Sara B. Algoe. "Stressful Life Events and Internalizing Symptoms in Emerging Adults: The Roles of Mindfulness and Gratitude." *Mental Health & Prevention* 12 (2018): 1–9. doi: 10.1016/J.Mhp.2018.08.003.

Ekman, Paul. "An Argument for Basic Emotions." *Cognition and Emotion* 6, no. 3-4 (1992): 169–200. doi: 10.1080/02699939208411068.

Emmons, Robert. *Thanks!: How Practicing Gratitude Can Make You Happier*. Boston, MA: Mariner Books, 2008.

Figley, Charles R. "Compassion Fatigue: Psychotherapists' Chronic Lack of Self Care." *The Journal of Clinical Psychology* 58, no. 11 (2002): 1433–1441. doi: 10.1002/Jclp.10090.

Gallagher, Stephen, Alejandro Castro Solano, and Mercedes Fernández Liporace. "State, But Not Trait Gratitude Is Associated with Cardiovascular Responses to Acute Psychological Stress." *Physiology & Behavior* 221 (2020). doi: 10.1016/J.Physbeh .2020.112896.

Gallegos, Autumn M., Megan C. Lytle, Jan A. Moynihan, and Nancy L. Talbot. "Mindful-ness-Based Stress Reduction to Enhance Psychological Functioning and Improve Inflammatory Biomarkers in Trauma-Exposed Women: A Pilot Study." *Psychological Trauma: Theory, Research, Practice, and Policy* 7, no. 6 (2015): 525–532. doi: 10.1037 /Tra0000053.

Gilbert, Paul. "Introducing Compassion-Focused Therapy." *Advances in Psychiatric Treatment* 15, no. 3 (2009): 199–208. doi: 10.1192/Apt.Bp.107.005264.

Greene, Joshua. *Moral Tribes: Emotion, Reason and the Gap Between Us and Them.* New York: Penguin Press, 2013.

Goleman, Daniel. *Emotional Intelligence: Why It Can Matter More Than IQ.* New York: Bantam Books, 1995.

Hermans, Dirk, Bernard Rimé, and Batja Mesquita. *Changing Emotions.* Psychology Press, 2013.

Hilton, Lara, Alicia R. Maher, Benjamin Colaiaco, Eric Apaydin, Melony E. Sorbero, Marika Booth, Roberta M. Shanman, and Susanne Hempel. "Meditation for Posttraumatic Stress: Systematic Review and Meta-Analysis." *Psychological Trauma: Theory, Research, Practice, and Policy* 9, no. 4 (2017): 453–460. doi: 10.1037/Tra0000180.

Hoffart, Asle, Tuva Øktedalen, and Tomas F. Langkaas. "Self-Compassion Influences PTSD Symptoms in the Process of Change in Trauma-Focused Cognitive-Behavioral Therapies: A Study of Within-Person Processes." *Frontiers in Psychology* (2015). doi: 10.3389/Fpsyg.2015.01273.

Hoge, Elizabeth A., Eric Bui, Luana Marques, Christina A. Metcalf, Laura K. Morris, Donald J. Robinaugh, John J. Worthington, Mark H. Pollack, Naomi M. Simon. "Randomized Controlled Trial of Mindfulness Meditation for Generalized Anxiety Disorder: Effects on Anxiety and Stress Reactivity." *The Journal of Clinical Psychiatry* 74, no. 8 (2013): 786–792. doi: 10.4088/JCP.12m08083.

Hoge, Elizabeth A., Eric Bui, Sophie A. Palitz, Noah R. Schwarz, Maryann E. Owens, Jennifer M. Johnston, Mark H. Pollack, and Naomi M. Simon. "The Effect of Mindfulness Meditation Training on Biological Acute Stress Responses in Generalized Anxiety Disorder." *Psychiatry Research* 262 (2018): 328–332. doi: 10.1016/J.Psychres.2017.01.006.

Kabat-Zinn, Jon. *Full Catastrophe Living: Using the Wisdom of Your Body and Mind to Face Stress, Pain, and Illness.* New York: Delacorte, 1990.

Kabat-Zinn, Jon, and Sharon Salzberg. *Loving-Kindness: The Revolutionary Art of Happiness.* Berkeley, CA: Shambhala Publications, 2004.

Kilpatrick, Dean G., Heidi S. Resnick, Melissa E. Milanak, Mark W. Miller, Katherine M. Keyes, and Matthew J. Friedman. "National Estimates of Exposure to Traumatic Events and PTSD Prevalence Using DSM-IV and DSM-5 Criteria." *Journal of Traumatic Stress* 26, no. 5 (2013): 537–547. doi: 10.1002/jts.21848.

Kini, Prathik, Joel Wong, Sydney McInnis, Nicole Gabana, and Joshua W. Brown. "The Effects of Gratitude Expression on Neural Activity." *Neuroimage* 128 (2016): 1–10. doi: 10.1016/j.neuroimage.2015.12.040.

Lawrence, Elizabeth M., Richard G. Rogers, and Tim Wadsworth. "Happiness and Longevity in the United States." *Social Science & Medicine* 145 (2015): 115–119. doi: 10.1016/J.Socscimed.2015.09.020.

Lee, Deborah A., and Sophie James. *The Compassionate-Mind Guide to Recovering from Trauma and PTSD: Using Compassion-Focused Therapy to Overcome Flashbacks, Shame, Guilt and Fear.* Oakland, CA: New Harbinger Publications, 2013.

Linehan, Marsha M. *Skills Training Manual for Treating Borderline Personality Disorder.* New York: Guilford, 1993.

Lush, Peter, Peter Naish, and Zoltan Dienes. "Metacognition of Intentions in Mindfulness and Hypnosis." (Report). *Neuroscience of Consciousness* 1 (2016): 1972–1932. doi: 10.1093/Nc/Niw007.

Mackenzie, Meagan B., Kayleigh A. Abbott, and Nancy L. Kocovski. "Mindfulness-Based Cognitive Therapy in Patients with Depression: Current Perspectives." *Neuropsychiatric Disease and Treatment* 14 (2018): 1599–1605. doi: 10.2147/NDT.S160761.

Maslow, Abraham H. "A Theory of Human Motivation." *Psychological Review* 50, no. 4 (1943): 370–396. doi: 10.1037/h0054346.

Morley, Richard H., and Cheryl Fulton. "The Impact of Mindfulness Meditation on Self-Esteem and Self-Compassion Among Prisoners." *Journal of Offender Rehabilitation* 59 (2020): 116–198. doi: 10.1080/10509674.2019.1697784.

National Center for PTSD. U.S. Department of Veterans Affairs. "How Common Is PTSD in Veterans?" Accessed November 22, 2020. PTSD.va.gov/understand/common/common_veterans.asp.

Pagni, Broc A., Melissa J. M. Walsh, Emily Foldes, Ann Sebren, Maria V. Dixon, Nicolas Guerithault, and B. Blair Braden. "The Neural Correlates of Mindfulness-Induced Depression Reduction in Adults with Autism Spectrum Disorder: A Pilot Study." *Journal of Neuroscience Research* 98, no. 6 (2020): 1150–1161. doi: 10.1002/Jnr.24600.

Papousek, Ilona, Karin Nauschnegg, Manuela Paechter, Helmut K. Lackner, Nandu Goswami, and Günter Schulter. "Trait and State Positive Affect and Cardiovascular Recovery from Experimental Academic Stress." *Biological Psychology* 83, no. 2 (2010): 108–115. doi: 10.1016/J.Biopsycho.2009.11.008.

Parsons, Christine E., Catherine Crane, Liam J. Parsons, Lone Overby Fjorback, and Willem Kuyken. "Home Practice in Mindfulness-Based Cognitive Therapy and Mindfulness-Based Stress Reduction: A Systematic Review and Meta-Analysis of Participants' Mindfulness Practice and Its Association with Outcomes." *Behaviour Research and Therapy* 95 (2017): 29–41. doi: 10.1016/J.Brat.2017.05.004.

Phillips, Cristy. "Lifestyle Modulators of Neuroplasticity: How Physical Activity, Mental Engagement, and Diet Promote Cognitive Health During Aging." *Neural Plasticity* (2017). doi: 10.1155/2017/3589271.

Rodak, Jourdan A. "PTSD's True Color: Examining the Effect of a Short-Term Coloring Intervention on the Stress, Anxiety and Working Memory of Veterans with PTSD." Master's Thesis at University of North Florida (2017). https://digitalcommons.unf.edu/cgi/viewcontent.cgi?article=1794&context=etd.

Rodríguez-Carvajal, Raquel, Carlos García-Rubio, David Paniagua, Gustavo García-Diex, and Sara de Rivas. "Mindfulness Integrative Model (MIM): Cultivating Positive States of Mind Towards Oneself and the Others Through Mindfulness and Self-Compassion." *Anales De Psicología/Annals of Psychology* 32, no. 3 (2016): 749–760. doi: 10.6018/Analesps.32.3.261681.

Rosenberg, Morris. *Society and the Adolescent Self-Image.* Princeton, NJ: Princeton University Press, 1965.

Salzberg, Sharon. "Mindfulness and Loving-Kindness." *Contemporary Buddhism* 12, no. 1 (2011): 177–182. doi: 10.1080/14639947.2011.564837.

Schreiner, Istvan, and James P. Malcolm. "The Benefits of Mindfulness Meditation: Changes in Emotional States of Depression, Anxiety, and Stress." *Behaviour Change* 25, no. 3 (2008): 156–168. doi: 10.1375/Bech.25.3.156.

Steptoe, Andrew, E. Leigh Gibson, Mark Hamer, and Jane Wardle. "Neuroendocrine and Cardiovascular Correlates of Positive Affect Measured by Ecological Momentary Assessment and by Questionnaire." *Psychoneuroendocrinology* 32, no. 1 (2007): 56–64. doi: 10.1016/J.Psyneuen.2006.10.001.

Tang, Yi-Yuan, Britta K. Hölzel, and Michael I. Posner. "The Neuroscience of Mindfulness Meditation." *Neuroscience* 16, no. 4 (2015): 213–225. doi: 10.1038/nrn3916.

Thompson, Brian L., and Jennifer Waltz. "Self-Compassion and PTSD Symptom Severity." *Journal of Traumatic Stress* 21 (2008): 556–558. doi: 10.1002/Jts.20374.

Tirch, Dennis, Laura R. Silberstein-Tirch, and Russell L. Kolts. *Buddhist Psychology and Cognitive-Behavioral Therapy: A Clinician's Guide.* New York: Guilford Press, 2015.

Tolle, Eckhart. *Stillness Speaks.* Novato, CA: New World Library, 2003.

World Health Organization (WHO). "Depression." January 30, 2020. Who.int /News-Room/Fact-Sheets/Detail/Depression.

Yang, Chuan-Chih, Alfonso Barrós-Loscertales, Meng Li, Daniel Pinazo, Viola Borchardt, César Ávila, and Martin Walter. "Alterations in Brain Structure and Amplitude of Low-Frequency After 8 Weeks of Mindfulness Meditation Training in Meditation-Naïve Subjects." *Scientific Reports* 9, no. 1 (2019). doi: 10.1038 /S41598-019-47470-4.

Zeng, Xianglong, Rong Wang, Vivian Y. L. Chan, Tian P. S. Oei, and Freedom Y. K. Leung. "The Four Immeasurables Meditations: Differential Effects of Appreciative Joy and Compassion Meditations on Emotions." *Mindfulness* 8, no. 4 (2017): 949–959. doi: 10.1007/s12671-016-0671-0.

INDEX

ACKNOWLEDGMENTS

All of us have a story, and mine would not be complete without Cesar and my family, amazing friends, colleagues, Zen community, and dogs. Thanks to all who have inspired me in my journey, especially Robert Kennedy Roshi.

ABOUT THE AUTHOR

 **Peter J. Economou, PhD, ABPP,** is an associate professor at Rutgers University in the Graduate School of Applied and Professional Psychology (GSAPP). He is the founder of a clinical practice specializing in cognitive and behavioral therapy (CBT) and sports psychology. He is licensed by NJ and NY to practice psychology, is board certified in CBT, and is a certified mental performance consultant (CMPC). Dr. Pete is also a student of Zen Buddhism, studying at the Morning Star Zendo with Robert Kennedy Roshi for several years, which has translated into his mindfulness practices offered through the third wave CBT. Listen to his podcast, *When East Meets West,* to learn more about the integration of CBT and Zen Buddhism.

Follow Dr. Pete:
Instagram: @officialdrpete
Twitter: @TheCWCNJ and @OfficialDrPete
Podcast: wheneastmeetswest.us

CPSIA information can be obtained
at www.ICGtesting.com
Printed in the USA
JSHW050529280121
11228JS00001B/3